I0801514

STORIES of NEW ORLEANS

by
Andre Cajun

Foreword By JOHN T. MAGILL

PELICAN PUBLISHING
New Orleans

To my beloved wife, Louise Navard

Copyright © 1941
By Andrew Jackson Navard

Copyright © 2013
By Pelican Publishing Company, Inc.
All rights reserved

First edition, 1941
First Pelican edition, 2013
Second Pelican printing, 2025

The word "Pelican" and the depiction of a pelican are trademarks of Arcadia Publishing Company Inc. and are registered in the U.S. Patent and Trademark Office.

ISBN: 9781455617784
E-Book ISBN: 9781455617791

AUTHOR'S NOTE

Lest it be forgotten, traditional history has superseded authentic or accepted history by many centuries. The writer's aim in the following pages is to keep alive for posterity Louisiana's traditional history. Whether or not the contents of this booklet is authentic the writer cannot say. It is given as gathered without the taking or adding of color, and it is hoped it will serve as intended until the light of truth dawns upon much of Louisiana's shadowed history.

Printed in the United States of America
Published by Pelican Publishing
New Orleans, LA
www.pelicanpub.com

Contents

Foreword

André Cajun—the self proclaimed "Sage of the Bayous"—first gave the world *Stories of New Orleans* in 1941. This was a time when the tallest buildings in the city were the Hibernia National Bank and American Bank. Big department stores and first-run movie palaces drew throngs of people to Canal Street. The French Quarter was only about two decades into its slow restoration and was still mostly ramshackle, run down, and not yet overcrowded with visitors. Tourism, however, was a growing business, but it was still nowhere near the economic engine it has become today. The big hotels of the day included the likes of the Roosevelt, St. Charles, Jung, and Monteleone. Antoine's, Galatoire's, Arnaud's, and Broussard's were already established parts of the French Quarter restaurant scene, while Bourbon Street had just begun its rise to party fame after Prohibition ended in 1933. There were Mardi Gras, although parades then only took place for about a week-and-a-half, and the Sugar Bowl that had begun in 1935, but there were few other events or festivals to entertain visitors or locals. Racial segregation at the time seemed as solid as a rock and banned blacks from most venues, and life-sized mammy dolls stood mutely promoting the sale of pralines in doorways of French Quarter souvenir shops.

During the 1940s and '50s André Cajun entertained readers with a series of booklet-sized historical parodies that tended to be convoluted, historically inaccurate, and obviously a product of his imagination. According to Cajun, they were drawn from local lore to humorously tell Louisiana's colorful and often controversial history.

Historical parody such as Cajun's is nothing new and remains popular today. Just a few years before publication of *Stories of New Orleans* the wildly popular *1066 and All That*—a parody of English history by W. C. Sellar and R. S. Yeatman—had taken the world by storm in 1930 and is still available. There have been historical movie and television parodies, such as Eddy Cantor's 1933 *Roman Scandals,*

"Peabody's Improbable History" segments on television's *Bullwinkle Show* in the 1960s, and screwball *Monty Python* movies of the '70s.

André Cajun was the pseudonym of Capt. Andrew Jackson Navard. *Stories of New Orleans* was among the earliest of his various publications which include titles like: *Louisiana Voodoo; Why Louisiana Has . . . Parishes, Police Jurymen, Red Bones, Creoles, Cajuns; Basin Street: Its Rise and Fall; Whisky, Pistols and Religion; Great Ghost Stories of Louisiana; Doctor of Honey Isle; The Pirate Lafite* [sic]; *Old Trenton on the Ouachita; Sage of the Bayous; Cleve Stewart; Bamboula Land; Earth's Oldest Feud; The Caul;* and *Ol' Nu'er 'leans Gumbo.* Each sold for a dollar or less including postage and could be found in book stores, souvenir shops, railroad station gift shops, news vendors, and any place where tourist items such as postcards and city maps could be found. A rare copy of the 1941 edition of *Stories of New Orleans* in the holdings of The Historic New Orleans Collection has the stamp of its vendor Old Town Praline & Novelty Shop, 627 Royal Street.

Andrew Jackson Navard was born in Lake Charles, Louisiana, in 1893. As a young man he was employed as a river pilot at the port of Lake Charles. About 1922, he moved to New Orleans where he worked as a Mississippi riverboat captain, which is how he received his moniker of captain. When he left this work he remained on the waters of the mighty Mississippi becoming a lecturer on the steamer *President*—a popular attraction docked at the foot of Canal Street that provided river tours and nightly dances. Here Navard must have enjoyed embellishing his yarns and historical parodies of Louisiana, which undoubtedly grew into the pages of the books he wrote. On August 6, 1957 after leaving his day's work on the *President*, Navard died without warning while entering his car, which was parked at the foot of Canal Street. He was only sixty-four years of age.

The 1941 edition of *Stories of New Orleans* was an un-illustrated paperback printed by the Press of Twin City Printing Company, Inc., in Monroe, Louisiana. It was "Dedicated to the thousands of Louisiana visitors who made it possible." The book must have sold very well, because it went into a number of enlarged editions. In

1945 it was published by Cajun Publishing Co. of New Orleans and this time was illustrated. It included a cartoonish cover drawing depicting an African American boy clinging to a moss-hung tree as he tried to avoid being attacked by an alligator. The comical yet racist theme of the cover is not unlike early twentieth-century postcards depicting similar subjects. Containing the same illustrations and cover, the book was republished in 1954 by Harmanson's Book Store in New Orleans. A reprint of this in August 1957—the time of Navard's death—reports it to be the eighth revision and enlargement as well as the ninth printing of *Stories of New Orleans.*

From earlier to later editions the table of contents had a few alterations. Chapters found in the 1941 edition, but not in the 1957 one, include "Lafitte and General Jackson," "Lafitte's Decision," and "The Rescue of Napoleon"—while in the later edition there are new chapters "Marie le Veau [*sic*], the Voodoo Queen," "Voodooism in Plaquemines Parish," and "The Brigham Young Courtyard."

André Cajun's publisher for many of his books was Joseph Shields Wilson Harmanson's book store on Royal Street. During the 1920s Harmanson, who was born in 1886, worked at Siler's book store at 1000 Canal Street where he was the store's vice president, but by the end of the Roaring '20s he and his wife established a book store of their own at 916 Gravier Street in the shadow of nearby financial district skyscrapers. In the early '30s Harmanson's moved to 333 Royal Street in the French Quarter specializing in secondhand and fine antiquarian books, as well as prints and painting and souvenirs. The shop served as a gallery for a number of the city's aspiring artists. The store was an iconic fixture in the city's literary and art world for nearly three decades until Harmanson's death on March 30, 1958.

Among the writers Harmanson published was Stanley Clisby Arthur probably best remembered for his 1936 book of French Quarter architectural walking tours entitled *Old New Orleans,* which has been very popular and has gone through numerous editions retaining its usefulness to this day. Other Harmanson publications included photography of Eugene Delcroix, a well known local photographer of the '40s. These were very straightforward books compared to André Cajun's humorous parodies, which were definitely in a different vein with little relevance to accurate history and with the presentation of basic histories through a white perspective of the early twentieth century.

Above all else Navard was a storyteller—a spinner of yarns—and he made no pretense about being an historian. His disclaimer in *Stories of New Orleans* informs the reader "Lest it be forgotten traditional history has superseded authentic or accepted history by many centuries. The writer's aim . . . is to keep alive for posterity Louisiana's traditional history. Whether or not the contents of this booklet is authentic the writer cannot say." In *Basin Street: Its Rise and Fall* Navard writes "The writer, dear reader, is a folklorist, not a historian and therefore does not pen history. . . . The aim herein is not to rattle any more bones of New Orleans' . . . past . . . the reader will note that the book is short, snappy and to the point." In *Whisky, Pistols and Religion* he reiterates that "The content herein is lore, not history. It is given as gathered without the adding or taking of color. It is written for entertainment and for those who care to do research on the territory mentioned."

André Cajun stories seem as if they may have been spread and elaborated on from one generation to the next by word of mouth, reaching the point where the stories were even believed. They certainly amuse—and even misinform unsuspecting newcomers unfamiliar with the state's history. In one such case in the early 1960s the writer of this foreword was told by a straight-faced individual that LaSalle named Louisiana in honor of King Louis XIV of France and Louis' wife Anna—although his wife at the time was actually named Maria Theresa. In *Why Louisiana Has . . .* Cajun tells a similar story, but he goes a step further by telling the reader that Louisiana was indeed named for Louis XIV, but Anna was "Anna Connena Comnerus, daughter of Alexius, an ancient ruler of the far east." Cajun explains that "Anna's writings had immense influence upon La Salle and he included her name in that of the state—Louisiana."

Navard's small histories are more often than not unashamedly racist, and he includes among his books titles *Has the Negro a History?*, and *Bleaching of the Black Race*. It can be argued that they are a product of his generation, because Navard's life spanned the years of Jim Crow segregation from his birth in 1893, three years before the United States Supreme Court in *Plessy v. Ferguson* upheld the doctrine of separate but equal, until his death in 1957 when school desegregation was rocking the south. There is no "political correctness" here—the term had not even been coined in Navard's lifetime. As a result, his stories of African Americans must be viewed as a product of conservative white attitudes in the American South during the first half of the twentieth century.

Although many of Cajun's white readers in the 1940s might have found his humorous references to race amusing, some seventy years later this provides a certain cringe-factor. While much of this may have been written without any deliberate malice on Navard's part, today it might stop the reader short in the same manner as cruel comic postcards or stereotypical motion picture depictions of non-whites in the 1930s—and these were accepted attitudes of the entire country. Today the books serve not only as an example of American racial attitudes of the day, but they also reveal how these have changed in the span of little more than half-a-century.

In *Stories of New Orleans,* Cajun points out with the long-term decline of the city that at the time of his writing it was the sixteenth largest city in the union, and he correctly adds that a hundred years earlier it was the third largest and was described then as "gay, dashing, full of charm and ambition to go forward." He describes the city as having been founded by the French, run by Catholics, owned by the Jews, and policed by the Irish. He adds that among African Americans, "It is also recorded by unwritten history that the Negro could not stand the combination" and with a "railroad ticket to Chicago, caused him to leave."

In Cajun's crazy quilt *Stories of New Orleans*, he plunges in by saying that the city was not founded by Bienville, but instead by his younger brother named Chateaugay who built a trading post on the site of the city years before Bienville even arrived. Chateaugay named it Crescent Port of Orleans in honor of the Duke of Orleans who financed the project.

Cajun was taken with pirates and inserts them into his history wherever possible. He made Chateaugay a pirate and said Crescent Port of Orleans was planned as "an outlet for pirate merchandise" becoming a successful trading spot by 1711. Chateaugay then moved his trading center to an area he called Barataria. Cajun said that Napoleon Bonaparte, whose body was "preserved in a cask of good English rum," was entombed—cask and all—in a Barataria cemetery.

Of the Spanish period, which lasted from the early 1760s until 1800, Cajun correctly identifies the surviving early architecture of the French Quarter as being Spanish, adding that when wealthy, Spanish-born Don Andres Almonester y Roxas financed rebuilding after the great fire of 1788 "The Don's only requirement was that the architecture be Spanish, and until this day it has remained Spanish." Cajun embellished the don's life by calling him governor of Louisiana—which he never was—and writing that he came to New Orleans on his honeymoon and his young bride made him stay here. However, in truth, Almonester arrived here as a widower and married a local girl six years later.

Spanish rule was unpopular with the French residents of New Orleans, and in another instance regarding this Cajun writes that following the death of Spain's King Charles III, "The French colonists, thinking Louisiana would again become a French possession. . . . The Spanish Governor Miro stopped this action, and for three years New Orleans was a pitiful place"—a choice of words not unlike something from *1066 and All That.*

In several instances Cajun uses Jackson Square as a meeting place for historically important people. In 1802 he has a pair of brothers named Kenneth David McOrr and Pressley Clinton McOrr sitting in the square and deciding upon joining the successful Barataria pirates, changed their names to Jean and Pierre Lafitte. Also in the square, Cajun has John McDonogh meet Abraham Lincoln, and McDonogh introduces the future president to a slave auction which so upsets Lincoln that he never returns to New Orleans.

McDonogh was one of the most successful and wealthiest merchants in New Orleans and Cajun puts him in contact with Barataria pirates, too. "Over many cups of coffee as strong as lye, black as night and hot as hell," McDonogh became the pirates' business agent enabling them to sail freely into the port of New Orleans. This merges pirate activity and legitimate business in New Orleans, which is not far from the truth, because smuggling was very big business in New Orleans during the territorial period between the Louisiana Purchase of 1803 and statehood in 1812 when both Lafitte and McDonogh were active in their respective trades.

Continuing his pirate story, Cajun also has Paul Tulane come to New Orleans to meet the pirate Lafitte at the latter's blacksmith shop, because as Tulane told Lafitte, he wanted to work in iron. Tulane eventually grew wealthy from working with the pirates and their gold enabled him to fund Tulane University. In an unlikely twist, Tulane also falls in love with Madame Delphine LaLaurie, infamous for torturing and killing slaves in her French Quarter mansion.

Aside from pirates, Cajun liberally sprinkles his tales with prostitutes and practitioners of Voodoo which, like the pirate Lafitte, were subjects of other booklets. Of Voodoo, Cajun writes that it originated in Africa and was practiced by the Israelites when they were slaves picking cotton for an Egyptian pharaoh. Moses delivered them from Voodoo, but it still managed to "spread to the Chaldeans, Druids and Magi," even though as Cajun says the Greeks "proved it a fraud."

In another meeting of characters Cajun has Marie Le Veau (his spelling) meet Gen. Ben Butler, the highly unpopular Federal commandant of New Orleans after the city's fall in the Civil War, nicknamed "Beast Butler." Cajun describes Butler in one vignette as "soaked in wine, smelling like a crate of sour grapes and two, teen-age octoroon girls pouring the general more wine." The general, according to Cajun, had soft spots for fine French wine and octoroons, and when he was plied with these treats, he gave permission for Marie Le Veau to hold "the western world's last greatest open Voo Doo ceremony." Like most whites in New Orleans in the early 1900s—and for many even to the present—Cajun held Benjamin Butler in the greatest disdain, but he does credit "Beast Butler" with cleaning up the city's filthy condition.

Even in the 1940s and '50s the defeat of Civil War and clashes of Reconstruction were still in the living memories of the most elderly white residents of the city. In the book, Cajun lashes out at the corrupt carpetbag rule and black Metropolitan Police for their "undisturbed plunder." He does not name the 1874 Battle of Liberty Place between the White League and Metropolitan Police, but he credits this armed battle on Canal Street for giving birth to the political organization of the Old Regulars which in Cajun's day "still exists."

Cajun shows more than a passing knowledge of New Orleans history and seems aware of its basics, but he embellishes and recreates wherever possible. He certainly does not let a few facts or chronology get in the way of his stream of historical consciousness. Those who know no better might take Cajun's spunky stories as fact, while those who are more aware of events might get a good laugh out of Cajun's historical misrepresentations. In its own way *Stories of New Orleans* and the other historical spoofs by André Cajun are products of their day in the American south that can still provide a few chuckles, as well as groans of disbelief. Pamela Arceneaux, Senior Librarian/Rare Books Curator of The Historic New Orleans Collection has succinctly described Cajun's books as "curiosities today."

John T. Magill
Curator/Historian, The Historic New Orleans Collection

The Founding of New Orleans

New Orleans, the South's greatest, America's most interesting and democracy's most unique city is the gateway to the South. It is the third city in the country in area, seventh in age, and fifteenth in population. It has the world's finest fresh water harbor and the cleanest thing around her skirts is the air she breathes. In dust particles per cubic foot New Orleans is the country's most immaculate city.

Traditionally, it is said that this quaint old city was not founded by Le Moyne de Bienville as is commonly believed, but found by him. Bienville's younger brother, Chateaugay, established and conducted a trading post on the site of New Orleans years before Bienville came into local history. The post bore the name of Crescent Post of Orleans in honor of the Duke of Orleans who financed Chateaugay's activities. Le Moyne de Iberville, the oldest brother of Bienville and Chateaugay, founded the present city of Mobile, Alabama, in 1701.

Some say Iberville had a character which was a cross between a preacher and a pirate. He would preach to his colonists when they needed it and would practice piracy for the same purpose. The latter he did when it was not too much of a risk to himself and his people. On the other hand, Chateaugay was carefree and was a pirate of first water. To danger and consequence he gave little thought. He did everything possible to persuade Iberville to turn Mobile into a freebooters' city. There is no doubt that Chateaugay's plans sounded sweet to the ears of Iberville, but the well garrisoned Spanish fort at Pensacola, Florida, prevented his yielding to the temptation. Realizing Iberville would never see things his way, Chateaugay sailed for France where he induced some of the older friends of the Duke of Orleans to finance his plans for a trading post which would serve as an outlet for pirate merchandise. The mental picture of pirate gold, precious stones, and large cargoes of valuable furs being transported from Mexico bound for Spain was vividly drawn. This, together with their own need for gold, soon gained for Chateaugay the financial backing he needed. He immediately sailed from France with the most motley crew of men that ever sailed the seas.

Chateaugay laid his plans well and followed them in order. He landed a little west of the mouth of the Mississippi river and established and named the community we know today as Barataria (meaning free trade).

To the Indians Chateaugay sent word that they could swap their furs and horses for powder and whiskey. To the pirates in the Mexican Gulf and the Caribbean Sea he sent word that they could swap their gold and merchandise for women and recreation with all safety to themselves. Under such inducements, Barataria rapidly became a post of importance.

To overcome the difficulty the Indians experienced in the swamps while going to and from Barataria, Chateaugay erected the post, Crescent of Orleans. Not only did the post serve this purpose, but solved the problem for inland business, as it had developed into a wholesale affair. This post was especially beneficial in the spring, when the Mississippi river flooded the swamps. Merchandise sent up the river was shipped by water to the post from Barataria, then transported by wagons to what is now Bayou St. John, where it was again loaded on boats and sailed to Springfield, La. From there wagon trains distributed it to the various parts of the interior.

The growth of Post Crescent of Orleans was almost as rapid as that of Barataria. It has been said that if

Chateaugay had not held its growth in check it would have outgrown both Barataria and Mobile. For several years Chateaugay commanded this post, handling enormous sums in gold, and valuable merchandise, apparently with very little trouble. He mixed Indians, pirates and Negroes in gambling games, cock fights and games of skill. He was master at all times, unrelenting to those who dared to oppose him, and always ruled with a cold heart.

If a pirate wanted an Indian's wife or daughter, he could have her for gold paid in advance. The husband or father was given whiskey until he became helpless. The pirate was then allowed the woman until the drunkard displayed signs of becoming sober. When he learned all that had happened and created a scene, he was given more whiskey and escorted from the post.

In the summer of 1711, Iberville came to the post and displayed orders from France that he was to take over the post, Crescent of Orleans. Chateaugay agreed without argument. Business at Barataria had grown so extensively he was needed there; then too, he did not relish a dispute with the French government. Chateaugay remained at the post long enough to notify the Indians and pirates that in the future all business would go to Barataria. He advised he would destroy the post because the French government desired to erect a fort on the site.

In the fall of 1711, Iberville built a fort; however, his plan to move Mobile to the location never materialized. Iberville was blamed for Chateaugay's leaving the post. The Indians hid in the long willow trees which grew in abundance around the fort and picked his men off with bow and arrow.

Iberville did not feel that Chateaugay was responsible for what the Indians did. He notified him that he was leaving the place for good. Chateaugay immediately returned to the post and things continued as of old.

In the spring of 1717, Chateaugay learned that another brother, Bienville, a gentleman and officer in the French King's navy, was on his way to erect a large fort on the site where his oldest brother had failed.

Bienville came February 9, 1718, and found the deserted post intact with large quantities of food, medicine and wine. The Indians asked the "new Frenchman"—their term for Bienville—"was he going to swap powder and whiskey for women. To the answer "no" the Indians shrugged their shoulders, cast sullen looks, departed into the swamp, and until the day, Kenneth David McOrr, better known as (Jean Lafitte the pirate) too possession of Barataria, persecuted the colonists.

The French Quarter

The New Orleans French Quarter consists of ninety-odd square blocks. It is bounded by Canal street on the south, Rampart street on the west, Esplanade avenue on the north, and the Mississippi river on the east. At one time three sides of the quarter were enclosed by a fourteen-foot wall made of bricks and cypress pilings; some fifty feet beyond the wall was a canal or moat. Each of the three walls had a gate; these gates were closed about dark and no one was allowed to leave or enter the Quarter without an order from the governor.

At what is today the corner of Canal and Royal streets was the location of one of the gates; Orleans and Rampart streets was the location of another, and the third gate was placed at Dauphine street and Esplanade avenue. All that remained of this wall was torn down after the Louisiana Purchase.

The buildings in the Quarter range in age from eighty-five to two hundred years, with the exception of eleven. A few of them have been renovated, some have been slightly repaired, and the remainder stand as erected. All are made of brick with roofs of slate and tile. The mortar is a combination of Mississippi river sand and finely broken clam shells. The brick came from Spain as ship ballast.

With the exception of one four-story building, they are one, two, and three stories. The buildings extend flush to the banquette or sidewalk. The ground floors are level with the banquette and are used for business, while the upper floors are used as living quarters. The rooms are large, with high ceilings, few have side windows and all have front windows extremely high, extending from the floor almost to the ceiling. On the outside is the shutter. As a rule, these shutters are kept closed. The walls are of plaster and the floor of cypress from one to two inches thick. In this climate of high humidity, the rooms are damp. Occasionally, the walls are so damp one cannot strike a match on them as is quite the custom. With the shutter always closed no sunlight can enter; this causes the room to be dark. This, however, seems to be most agreeable to the Spanish for they go so far as to claim that such a condition is healthful. When one takes into consideration the city's once high tubercular rate, one would not think so.

Most of the buildings have little or no yard. Some have a two-foot alleyway floored with flag-stones. Between the edge of the flagstones and the property line runs a small ditch which, in the early days was used to convey sewerage from the water closet into the gutter in the street.

Each building has a balcony for each story, some as wide as the banquette, others half. The banister or railing is of iron grille, some cast, some hand wrought by slave labor. Many and varied are the designs, including lace, fruit, birds, foliage, and occasionally, the coat of arms of the House of Bourbon.

These balconies are used for many different purposes. Some are converted into flower gardens, others used as washing sheds. To the native it is not unusual, even today, to see sheep and goats quartered on the balconies.

Some of the buildings have beautiful court yards, with the partition fences, which are brick walls, covered with ivy and wisteria. In the corners are large palms with long, graceful fronds. Around the foot of the walls are beds of annuals. The background of dark green foliage, which enhances the riot of color, lends much charm to the atmosphere of the court yard. This beauty does not apply to all, for there are courtyards which make a city dump look like a footstool for angels.

The streets are narrow and their first pavement was cobblestones. Prior to this the streets were practically impassable in wet weather. Today the streets are just as narrow and possibly a lot more tiresome to travel. Electric cars use the center; a large truck is forced to back in order to turn the corners, sight-seeing cars drive slowly. All this tends to make the native detour the Quarter.

Today this section of the city is still called the French Quarter. In reality it should be Spanish, for the city as it had been erected by the French, with the exception of two buildings, was destroyed by fire Good Friday morning, 1788. As this was a religious holiday and it was against the law of the Roman church to sound a bell on Good Friday, the fire alarm was not given. A strong east wind fanned the flames and the fire gained such headway that by the time the people were aware of it, the fire had gotten beyond control. In this manner the old French city erected by Bienville soon became a city of the past. There has not been another such great fire in the city since.

The French Quarter at that time was practically all of New Orleans and was under Spanish rule. France was in the process of preparing the French people for a revolution and cared little about what happened to the colony. The Spanish, on the other hand, were deeply interested and after learning of what was going to eventually happen in France, prepared to rebuild the city. Under Spanish rule building was slow. From 1788 to 1794 the city had no church or public buildings. The people lived in tents and palmetto huts. Governor Miro did all possible. He even went so far as to lift trade restrictions in order to prevent a threatened famine.

Early in March New Orleans received word that Charles III, King of Spain, had passed on. The French colonists, thinking Louisiana would again become a French possession, revived their old interest. The Spanish Governor Miro stopped this action, and New Orleans for three years was a pitiful place.

In 1791, Spain sent a new governor, an aged wealthy Spanish nobleman, Don Andreas Almonaster. The trip from Spain to New Orleans was a honeymoon for the Don and his recently married youthful wife who made his stay in New Orleans a honeymoon which proved most beneficial to the colonists. The Don was not only liberal with his government's money, but his own also. The long desired building program got under way. He let the people have their choice about what, how, and where to build. The Don's only requirement was that the architecture be Spanish, and until this day it has remained Spanish.

The name French Quarter was applied by the incoming Americans after the Louisiana Purchase. No one knows why the term has been able to survive the years when, in reality, the Quarter is Spanish in architecture, more Spanish is spoken, and the majority of the customs are of Old Spain.

Jackson Square

Jackson Square is the civic center of New Orleans. Around the square is entwined the city's religious, social and political history. The original name of the square was Place d'Armes, meaning the reviewing of troops. It was there Bienville reviewed the troops as they landed to establish the city he called New Orleans. This name remained until February 12, 1815, when the Creole girls of the city, in the square crowned General Andrew Jackson the hero of the Battle of New Orleans. Upon the suggestion of these girls the name was changed to Jackson in honor of the general.

In the center of the square stood the official flagpole for the Mississippi Valley. Up and down its smooth weather-beaten surface traveled five different flags. On December 20, 1803, the French flag was lowered, never to rise again as a territorial flag in these United States.

The square has always been a gathering place regardless of one's social standing, creed or color. It served as a retreat for lovers and its first romance happened in

1728, when the Casquette girls were handed out to the unattached men of the colony for wives.

All the city's business for the first hundred years was transacted in the Square, illegal as well as legal. Many dark plots were hatched in the shadows of a willow or an orange tree, the first foliage of the square.

There captains of pirate ships met honest merchants and disposed of their cargoes; likewise narcotic agents met buyers; many murderers and suicides stayed in the Square and meditated until they worked up sufficient courage to execute their plans. Arrangements for numerous duels were completed in the Square, but none were ever fought there. Occasionally there was a fist fight which was stopped immediately as the natives have always looked upon Jackson Square as a place somewhat sacred. Although all manner of evil was generated and harbored there, the natives kept it below the surface. At no time was anything permitted to disturb the harmony and tranquility of the Square. More schemes for making easy money and plans for the extermination of people have been born in the Square than any other spot its size in the country.

In the year 1802, two brothers, Kenneth David and Pressley Clinton McOrr, sat in the Square and decided they would cast their lot with the pirates of Barataria, and make the business of piracy a paying proposition. Two years later these brothers were known in the Square as Jean and Pierre Lafitte.

In the year 1831, John McDonogh and Abraham Lincoln stopped in the Square while McDonogh explained how one could tell a free Negro from a slave. The first high-jacking, as a business, in the country was planned in the Square. It was there a Portuguese ship captain made a deal with a planter who hired out his slaves. Upon completion of the job, the captain forced the slaves aboard and sailed for Pensacola where he sold them.

The Square has not always been the beauty spot it is today. For one hundred and twenty-eight years it was a bog hole. The benches, which were but-ends of cypress logs, floated all over the Square when it rained. The Baroness of Pontalba, a wealthy Spanish noblewoman, decided she would eliminate this eye-sore. With the help of friends she purchased bricks and built a wall two feet high around the Square and filled it in, and trees, shrubs and flowers were set out. Shortly thereafter Clark Mills' $20,000 bronze equestrian monument of General Andrew Jackson (Old Hickory) was placed in the Square. On May 7, 1862, the Yankee General Benjamin Butler had inscribed on the base of the monument, "The Union must and shall be preserved."

New Orleans has sixty-three squares or parks, but Jackson Square is the crowning jewel of them all.

Old Orleans

New Orleans, according to tradition, was founded by the French, run by the Catholics, owned by the Jews, and policed by the Irish. For these reasons if no other it has less Negro population than any other large Southern city. It is also recorded by unwritten history that the Negro could not stand this combination. This, together with his desire for a new suit of clothes, a gold watch and a railroad ticket to Chicago, caused him to leave.

The average Southern white man thinks that because New Orleans is a great seaport it has a large number of Orientals. In this they are mistaken, as their number will not exceed five hundred. Yet New Orleans is a very cosmopolitan city, for all the major languages of the world have been spoken within her boundaries.

The laws of that old city have always been in favor of the aristocrat. This does not mean, neither is it intended to imply, that New Orleans does not have a large heart, for she is most charitable toward her unfortunate. Up until the last few years the city was selfish in this respect, for only the natives could get this relief.

Bienville, a French Canadian, mapped out the city. This map called for ten thousand people, no more. Beyond this number no welcome was to be extended. Under this restriction the city's growth was slow, and to those who did not speak French or Spanish she gave wide berth socially.

In the year 1803, when the fascinating old city became the property of the United States Government, she became over-run with visitors from the East. The natives called these visitors foreigners and openly insulted them. This attitude waxed strong until after the Battle of New Orleans, at which time the natives relented and business took a turn for the better. This, however, was another cause for slow growth.

In 1819 the first Protestant church (Prebyterian) was established. Free Masons wore their emblems in public without insults and ceased holding their meetings in the swamps outside the city limits.

Louisiana entered the Union April 12, 1812, as a state. It was not until 1821 that New Orleans gained the reputation of being a business center of the country. Ships flying flags of all nations lined her waterfront, trade was brisk and grew more brisk with each passing month.

In 1840, we find New Orleans the third city in the country in population and first in commerce. At this time her people were enjoying life, drinking good whiskey, gambling heavily and selling her black women for one dollar per pound. Her young golden, amber skinned women, of whom it was said, were so imbounded in love that flowers withered more quickly in their hands than any other woman from the seed of man, sold at from five to eight dollars a pound.

Such was New Orleans in 1840—gay, dashing, full of charm and ambition to go forward. Was this not true of all the world, for each nation was at peace with the other and only beasts and savages were fighting. Napoleon Bonaparte lay dead, cramped but preserved in a cask of good English rum, his body intact except for his bowels, which had been cast into the sea. His body, cask and all, safely entombed in a Baratarian cemetery.

This reign of peace was not for long. Already the goddess of strife and jealousy had noticed the earth was not offering her usual sacrifice, and set into motion plans to bring some parts of the earth to her altar.

The first inkling New Orleans received of these plans was brought to her by an Ohio steamboat captain, who told along the riverfront that in the East a party had been formed, called Abolitionists, whose object was to free the Negro. New Orleans laughed, drank, and shook her dice harder and otherwise entertained the idea as ridiculous. But not for long. Soon her trade began to drop off, her visitors became fewer and their stay shorter. The discovery of gold in California in 1849 climaxed her growth and New Orleans began to fall back. In the past hundred years she has fallen to the fifteenth city in population.

This loss, many believed, was due first to her political situation, second, her citizens traveled little and third, the aristocracy opposed education of the poor. Today, if one took time to search the cold ashes of that once burning fire of resentment, he would find the city has one of the country's finest municipal school systems where the poor have opportunities equal to those of the wealthy.

The ten years between 1850 and 1860 were lean years for New Orleans. Wagon trains from Chicago and St. Louis took her river trade, strangers ceased to enter her gates and spend large sums for a change of air and love. For they, too, followed the wagon trains. The merchants missed this trade and imports began to fall off.

A remedy for this financial slump was sought. A group of citizens met and formed an organization they called the Chamber of Commerce. These men made strenuous efforts to regain at least a part of the business which the city had lost. This august body worked long and hard trying to dress business in a way she would be attractive. When they discovered the only suitable raiment for business was sackcloth, they gave up. To make matters worse, the beautiful women who gave to New Orleans the restful atmosphere the tired planters loved, set up a terrific howl when they found they were unable to replace their worn silk gowns. They at first consulted that august body, the Chamber of Commerce, and left in disgust, purchased plaster images and prayed until their knees became calloused. The black clouds of poverty hung like a great tent over the city. So concerned were her people they failed to notice the Yellow Jack which had slipped into her midst. Its coming brought upon the city a far greater calamity than the lack of American goods. The old "hussy" as the city is often called, survived the ordeal as she had other visits of Yellow Jack. She shook her head, purged her politics, material self and lent an ear to the low far-off rumblings of war talk, civil war, the most horrible of all wars known to man. Being pleasure bent, her ear soon tired of that which was not generated by exotic pleasure.

During the years 1850 to 1860 New Orleans was practically a forgotten city. The singing of the Negroes along the riverfront turned from songs of amusements to those of mournful chants. Merchants pulled their hair, prostitutes cursed their old plaster images and purchased new ones.

Christmas of 1860 was the poorest New Orleans ever celebrated. Her only hope, it was believed, lay in a new president, a change in National leadership would be beneficial to her. In part, this was true. The year 1861 had hardly dawned before trade began to reappear on the river, busness shed its sackcloth, the prostitutes threw their plaster images out the windows and New Orleans became its old self again.

The rolling of dice in the Royal street gambling resorts, the drinking of absinthe in the coffee houses, so dimmed the low rumblings of civil war that her people, wrapped in the whirl of pleasure, failed to hear or heed the "black talk" which was slowly engulfing the Nation.

John McDonogh

John McDonogh, a Scotch Irishman, and founder of the present school system of New Orleans, was born in Baltimore in 1779. He came to New Orleans in 1800. He was historically known as a hermit, miser, bachelor and philanthropist, a queer combination.

He came to New Orleans at the age of 21 as the representative of an Eastern shipping company. Due, however, to the pirates that infested the Caribbean Sea and the Mexican Gulf, few of the ships of his firm reached port intact. Most of them reported cargoes looted, with part of their crews missing. This left McDonogh with much idle time. Naturally, his thoughts turned to pirates. Where would be the logical place for the pirates, especially those operating in the Mexican Gulf, to dispose of their loot?

The more McDonogh thought of this the more he was convinced that this loot was coming into New Orleans, not via Barataria, as many believed, for were not the Baratarians too poor to buy anything? In fact, all New Orleans had received from Barataria in the last few years was fish, shrimp, crabs and calls for help.

McDonogh decided there was only one way to solve this problem and solve it he would. Immediately he gave up his swanky apartment on Toulouse street and moved into a shabby, ordinary room on Decatur street. He dressed in the garb of a muskrat parish trapper, sauntered up and down the levee and talked with all who could be engaged in conversation. McDonogh not only found the answer to his problem, but learned much more. He met several captains of pirate ships, and soon discovered all of them were disappointed and concerned about the way affairs at Barataria had turned.

Into an ill-lighted corner of the Old French Market coffee stand, McDonogh gathered these pirate captains. Over many cups of coffee as strong as lye, black as night and hot as hell, McDonogh suggested to these gentlemen of the black flag they needed a business agent in New Orleans. To this they all agreed, but where could they find a man sufficiently educated and trustworthy to represent them. Finally, after much effort McDonogh convinced these pirate captains that he was the man. After much talk pro and con, a satisfactory agreement with all concerned was reached.

Immediately thereafter, these captains sailed their ships into the harbor of New Orleans and docked at her wharves, discharged their cargoes and took on supplies like any honest merchant ship. This business, under the guiding hand of McDonogh, grew by leaps and bounds—and likewise his wealth.

McDonogh's wealth floated him into the swim of the gay social life of New Orleans. As he was a good talker and the best dressed man in the city he soon anchored himself in his social position. On the downtown lake corner of Chartres and Toulouse streets he erected one of the finest homes in the French Quarter. Here he entertained in the style of newly acquired wealth. To give his home the real social atmosphere of the day, he purchased several beautiful young octoroon girls and soon gained the reputation of being a gay and dashing blade. The Creole belle considered it a very great honor to receive an invitation to a McDonogh courtyard dance.

It was during one of these dances that McDonogh met the only woman he ever loved. To impress her, he spent money freely and lavished expensive gifts upon her. Although he entertained nightly and filled social engagements during the day, he never neglected his duty to the pirates, or failed to keep a political ear to the ground.

Rumors from Washington had reached New Orleans that the Federal government was planning an embargo act. McDonogh knew that if this act was passed his connection with the pirates must cease. If such was to be, he could no longer place contraband in public warehouses to be sold in competition with legitimate business. The louder the talk upon the embargo act, the greater became McDonogh's desire to sever all his connections with the pirates. Never would the pirates accept the embargo act as an excuse for his withdrawal. Fate served him a good turn and relieved him of his worry in the form of a chance acquaintance, a man by the name of Kenneth David McOrr.

One day this gentleman appeared in his office and introduced himself as Jean Lafitte, governor of Barataria. He also informed McDonogh that he was to take over his activities with the pirates in its entirety. McDonogh looked

Lafitte over from head to foot and to himself said, "This is something heaven has sent."

McDonogh celebrated his easy release with a grand party and dance. Many expensive wine glasses were chipped and broken that night. On the second floor of McDonogh's home his pumpkin-skinned octoroon girls entertained a chosen few of the young blades with a hay market circus and a Bamboula dance.

McDonogh had long looked forward to the day when he could forget pirates, for upon that day he could ask a certain young lady to become Mrs. McDonogh. But this time, as the tradition goes, fate did not smile favorably upon him. For some reason (still unknown) the young lady rejected McDonogh's hand in marriage. Some said it was because McDonogh was Protestant and she was Catholic. Others said it was because McDonogh would not agree to dispose of his beautiful octoroon girls. Whatever the reason, be that as it may, McDonogh gave up his Chartres home and friends. He purchased a plantation across the river and the gay life of New Orleans saw McDonogh no more.

For forty years McDonogh lived as a hermit, miser, and bachelor seemingly with but one ambition—that of amassing money. Money flowed to him like water to the sea. He bought anything he could get at his price and developed the first successful three-ball (pawnbroker) business in New Orleans. He became a power in the bank of Lafitte and loaned money at exorbitant rates of interest, but only on security that his Satanic Majecty would accept. It was said of him that "he would jump the fence to save the hinges." McDonogh's desire for power controlled by money could not be denied.

In the later years of his life, when he walked the streets of New Orleans he was hissed by the children, who shouted, "McDonogh, the Miser!" They threw stones at him and laughed at his shabby clothes. For this treatment McDonogh showed no signs of resentment. Occasionally he would look up when tormented, smile, and pass on.

Jean Lafitte was the only man McDonogh had respect for, otherwise he was friendless.

McDonogh was one of America's farsighted men. Years before it came, he foresaw the emancipation of the Negro. In order that he might not be caught with thousands of dollars invested in Negro flesh, he executed a plan whereby his Negroes could buy their freedom at no loss to himself.

When McDonogh died in 1850, he divided his fortune, about two million dollars, between the cities of New Orleans and Baltimore for educational purposes. In his will he stipulated that the Bible be read once daily in the New Orleans public schools. The boys and girls from the fifth grade up must be segregated, the first Friday in May should be known as McDonogh Day, and all public school children should come to his grave, sing songs and cast garlands of flowers.

Later, when his remains were removed to Baltimore, the public school children erected a monument to his memory. It is there the children today cast their garlands of flowers.

Because of McDonogh's generosity, and the honesty and wisdom of those people who have handled these funds, New Orleans today, this writer believes, has one of America's finest municipal school systems. Although McDonogh died hated and despised by those who knew him, he redeemed himself in death, and today his memory is honored above all others of the Crescent City.

General Andrew Jackson

Late in the summer of 1814, General Andrew Jackson, in a whirlwind campaign, completely crushed the Creek Indians. Very much elated, the General, with his army of about 2,000 men, established headquarters at Mobile, Ala. There he waited for Washington to appropriate the necessary funds to proceed against the Seminole Indians of Florida who persisted in making war outside of Spanish territory.

Summer passed, fall came; still no funds had been received. General Jackson's elation turned into worry, for winter was coming and his army was in rags, with food scarce. To make bad matters worse, the fall rains had set in. Many of the soldiers became ill with chills and fever. Peruvian Bark, as quinine at that time was called, was hard to get. For it was not until 1816 that the medical profession recognized quinine as valuable in combating malaria.

Thanksgiving Day, 1814, General Jackson became ill with chills and fever. He was confined to his two-room, Negro plantation-shack which served as his quarters. His body servant, an old Negro man who had followed the General through many campaigns, kept a roaring fire in the old fashioned fireplace. Fully dressed, General Jackson sat before the fire with a blanket thrown around him. Shaking like a leaf, he cursed every official in Washington and blamed them for the present predicament of the army.

The old Negro servant was the busiest man that ever trod Alabama soil. For now his duties were not only to watch the General and see that he did not catch fire from the sparks which flew from the pine knots, but to deliver orders to army officers who were ill, the hardest task of all was to listen to his master curse the Indians, Washington, himself, and everyone in general, between chills.

Such was the condition of General Jackson and his army on the last night of November, 1814. A howling, northeast wind accompanied with heavy rains was rocking the cabin. The mud between the logs became loose and fell, leaving openings through which the wind and rains came.

As usual, the General sat before the fire, his gaunt frame shaking with a chill, while the old Negro was busy hanging blankets on the walls to shut out the wind, in an effort to prevent the General from becoming "rechilled," as he said. While so engaged, a knock came upon the door. Upon opening the door, a sentry saluted, and announced a rider from New Orleans with important dispatches from Governor Claiborne. The rider stepped forward and handed to Jackson the letters and information that Jean Lafitte, the Baratarian Pirate had sent to Governor Claiborne. Twelve thousand well-armed and well-trained British soldiers were in the Mexican Gulf under two able generals, Pakenham and Gibbs, and they planned to attack New Orleans.

This information so astounded Jackson that he forgot his chills and began raving. He cursed Washington, the British, and the audacity of that Pirate Lafitte. He suddenly stopped his flow of profanity, faced the three men, and told them his first act upon reaching New Orleans would be to hang that contemptible Pirate Lafitte to the first suitable cypress tree he could find.

Without another word, General Jackson dismissed the rider with instructions to Governor Claiborne to send all the Peruvian Bark available and he would be in New Orleans as soon as as he was able to ride.

Some two weeks passed before Jackson could make the trip to New Orleans. This trip he made alone on horseback, accompanied by his body servant, who rode a mule. Due to the mule's gait and stubbornness, the General lost his temper on more than one occasion; however, when not so engaged, he was in high spirits.

He told his old Negro how quick he would expel the British. New Orleans was not only a large city but a rich one, and he would have no difficulty in equipping his army and enlisting more men. The British disposed of, he would announce that he would be a candidate for the Presidency of the United States. Being a national hero, he would be elected by a large majority, then he would dress Rachel in white, take her to Washington, serve one term, then retire as a corporation lawyer, so planned General Jackson as he rode into New Orleans.

Still ill with fever, practically penniless, he went directly to Governor Claiborne. Jackson had only twenty dollars to his name, and in commemoration of this incident we find Jackson's portrait upon the $20 bank note today.

Governor Claiborne shattered all his ambitions when he told Jackson the city had no money and its credit was in bad shape. To add to his dismay, he was further advised that the city had few men who were physically able to become soldiers. The General could proclaim martial law and confiscate everything available but unless he could get help from Washington this would be useless.

These few words from Governor Claiborne so stunned General Jackson he was unable to speak. For a minute he leaned heavily upon his old darky, who was always by his side. With the Governor's words ringing in his ears his thought reverted to his boyhood days when a British officer during the American Revolution slapped him across the face with the broad side of his sword, marking him for life. Here, again, the British were taking from him his long cherished ambition, that of becoming President and Rachel would still be the wife of a Cumberland River shanty-boat general.

Those who witnessed this incident, as the tradition goes, said that Jackson was the most pitiful man they had ever seen.

In ragged clothes, his body racked with fever, he indeed was a pitiful sight. The General soon regained his poise, took a step nearer the Governor, shook his bony finger in his face, and said angrily, "Bring to me Mr. Lafitte, the Gentleman from Barataria, the only one outside of the Almighty God who has the power to save this Nation."

The General turned abruptly and left Governor Claiborne. Leaning upon his old Negro, Jackson was escorted to his headquarters on the uptown river corner of St. Louis and Chartres streets, and there waited for Lafitte the Pirate.

The Battle of New Orleans

December 20, 1814, was an unusually warm day for New Orleans. The cold wave which had chilled the city for three weeks had given way to south winds which brought the warmth her citizens loved.

That night the Creoles were celebrating with a ball given in honor of the eleventh anniversary of the Louisiana Purchase. Despite the fact that the British were hammering at the city's back door, threatening her very existence, the event looked most promising. General Jackson, commander of the city's defense, was in deep conference with his old darky, planning ways and means to make his uniform presentable for the evening. Although he had but recently been a very sick man, thanks to Lafitte's Peruvian bark, he was now feeling much better.

The General, like the natives, for the time put the British out of his mind, and entered into the spirit of the ball. He told his old Negro servant he felt so "fit" that he wished Mrs. Jackson could be with him to attend. Few events, if any, would have given Jackson more pleasure than to enter the ballroom with Rachel on his arm. As this could not be, he would enter upon the arm of Lafitte.

General Jackson, in full uniform, sat by his bedroom window sipping coffee and waiting the arrival of Lafitte. He noticed a man running up the street, and heard him ask the sentry in an excited voice to permit him to see the General. Jackson waited to hear no more. He met the man halfway on the stairs. From this messenger Jackson learned the British were in Lake Borne, trying to locate a suitable place for landing. Jackson immediately issued orders to the messenger and a score of others to report to the place where the British were seen, with instructions to advise him hourly of the British activities.

Another messenger was dispatched to the old Absinthe House, one of the city's favorite coffee houses, for Lafitte. Lafitte came at once, and when given the message advised Jackson that there was no need for alarm. Lafitte explained that his men would see that the British would become confused after entering the swamp. Once in the swamp, with the help of the mosquitoes, the British would be easy to handle. Lafitte suggested that they attend the ball and say nothing to the natives about the affair.

December 21 and 22 passed; New Orleans remained quiet. Still the news that the British were landing troops on the shores of Lake Borne was withheld from the natives. Jackson prepared a thousand men to leave at a moment's notice. The British, some five thousand in number, had avanced into the swamp for two miles, their progress slow and the mosquitoes bad.

Shortly after midnight December 22, 1814, Jackson sent a thousand men into the swamp. From the noise these men made the British believed they were out-numbered and retreated, leaving behind small cannons and other equipment to sink into the mud.

Again, on New Year's Day, 1815, Jackson's men met and scattered the British.

The Battle of New Orleans occurred about two miles below the city on the Chalmette Plantation. At that time a narrow, crooked bayou ran through this plantation, extending from the river to the lake. It had been straightened and deepened by swampers who used it to float timber into the river. Fortunately, the mud from this bayou had been thrown on the New Orleans, or the north side.

This created a levee about four feet high. Lafitte advised Jackson to make his stand behind this levee.

Following this suggestion, Jackson piled bales of cotton on top of the levee. From behind this breastworks was fought the shortest and most decisive battle ever fought upon American soil. As this is a traditional story, the writer will omit all that history records.

Upon the suggestion of Lafitte, Jackson lined his men seven deep, one behind the other, for the entire length of the levee, a distance of about one and one-quarter miles, with specific instructions for the first line to fire, step back, re-load, and fall in line. No one was to fire until the signal was given and only when a red coat could be seen. The slogan along the line of battle was, "Make every shot tell; we do not have war ships loaded with ammunition."

The immortal day, January 8, 1815, broke warm and foggy. Silent as a tombstone, the Americans lay behind their entrenchment, while the noise of the British movement made their plans plain. They were advancing slowly over the soft turf, cursing the people who lived upon such soil.

As though some fairy waved her magic wand over the battlefield, the wind suddenly freshened from the north. The fog lifted. The British could be seen about a quarter of a mile off, their line out of order, men struggling with artillery trying to drag it through the mud, officers on horseback cursing their mounts because they were unable to run. They immediately reformed their ranks and began an artillery bombardment.

Jackson went up and down his line, telling his men to hold their fire, for, as Lafitte said, with every shot the British artillery sank deeper into the mud. In this manner the British were forced to abandon their artillery and advance with muskets.

At this time, Jackson issued an order similar to that of Marion, the Swamp Fox of the Carolinas: "Don't fire until you can see the cross belts."

When the British were within a hundred yards, Jackson gave the order to fire. The sharpshooters from Kentucky and Tennessee centered their fire upon the officers, the army poured rifle fire and the Baratarians cannon fire into the oncoming ranks of the British. As they knew nothing of fighting an enemy they could not see, the British wavered, staggered, and fell back, leaving many of their number on the field. They reformed their ranks and advanced again to meet with the same result. They made the third advance and this time retreated in utter confusion. It is said that this was the most disgraceful retreat ever made by a British army.

The battle ended with the American losses only fifty-six, the British over two thousand.

The result of this battle displayed to the world the might and power of the United States.

Except for a shaft 106 feet high, there is no marker on this battlefield. Today it is a place where cattle graze.

King of Basin Street

Basin Street

"Her sins be forgiven for she hath loved much." Basin Street! Seven blocks long and, in its day, each block a gold mine, and for a hundred and three years the main thoroughfare of the notorious red-light district of New Orleans. While reading this it might be well to remember: the dry and wrinkled raisin was once a virtuous grape and the hardest debt the human being has to pay is for the contamination of his or her holy temple—the body.

Basin Street, and the foulness that laid behind it—west—women of all ages, races, creeds and colors traded body for gold, and men their cash for pains later in the liver.

In the early history of New Orleans the inhabitants, who were not members of the Upper Crust, referred to the French Quarter as God's portion of the Dear Isle of

Orleans. When they wished to fill in low places about their property, they would go a few hundred yards west of what is now North Rampart Street for the necessary filling. This constant hauling away throughout the years caused a depression which, when it rained, became a pond of water or, as the French termed it, a "Basin."

Early in the fall of 1814 word sprang up and down the Ohio and Mississippi Valley that General Andrew Jackson and his two thousand "mosquito-bitten, dirty-shirt" soldiers were on their way to New Orleans where they were to be paid, including all back pay due them. Washington, D. C., it seems, let out the word "Unpaid soldiers do not fight as well as those who are," and, if the British were as strong as General Jackson believes they were, it would be the logical time to pay the soldiers.

To the ears of the prostitutes along the Ohio and Mssissippi river ports it was sweet talk. They disposed of all but their personal possessions, and by flatboats, broadhorn, buckboard, buggy, horseback and on foot they flocked to New Orleans like Hell's sins to the first garden.

Many of the soldiers and some of the inhabitants gave the harlots a hearty welcome. But the Crust of God's portion cast them out. These women of all ages, color, description, and disease, were a lot hard of hand and heart, and did not for a moment hesitate to remind the "Crust" that the Louisiana Purchase had made them purchased property.

With some soldier help and timber, pilfered by river rats from the waterfront, the prostitutes erected shacks upon short poles in the Basin, dug a drainage ditch to carry away the water, and hung out red lights that remained until 1917.

The Crust of God's portion—particularly the women—afire with keen curiosity to know first hand what was going on in what they chose to call "Satan's portion of the

Isle of Orleans" went first to their chosen house of prayer where they wrestled mightily in invocation for an advance forgiveness for gazing upon such an unholy place, and then ventured as far as North Rampart Street, but no further, most probably because of the mud. And there, in wild-eyed astonishment, gazed upon the nation's first nudist colony. Curiosity satisfied to capacity, they hurried back to their particular sanctuary for another mighty bout with prayer, forgetting the Biblical—Hosea 4:14.

Like frightened sheep the ladies pleaded with the holy men to do something to rid the city of such an unholy, vile, unhallowed place. The holy men's efforts, however, were as useless as the knowledge of a new-born babe. The sale of Louisiana had stripped them of the iron glove, leaving the bare hand which, in such matters, is as ineffective as a rope of sand.

While waiting for an answer to their prayers—"The holy men grew in strength." Hell's portion of the Dear Isle of Orleans was growing like grass on a Democrat's farm.

It was not, however, until the coming of the steamboat and the immense increase in river trade—also in harlots— that the prostitutes were able to do anything about the sanitary conditions under which they were forced to live. Fearing the swamp which lay to the rear (west) of them, they huddled into a little knot, and there remained, until the new spurt in river trade gave them the financial and moral support they so badly needed to to expand.

Voodoo doctors with their weird chants, drum beats and custom of releasing giant birds, black in color with large wings and yellow on the underside, from the swamp each Friday night to fly low over the harlots' shacks and vomit upon persons as well as housetops, placed mortal fear in many of these women. When the opportunity did come they vacated in a hurry. Those with more gall than reasoning muscled in on the Irish Channel, a new annex to God's portion of the city, paralleling the river, two blocks west, extending from Canal Street south to what is now Louisiana Avenue. And there, for eighty years they fought to maintain their place in the sun in this particular community.

When the day of moving did arrive they left like they came—overnight. The more peaceful of them went back to Basin Street where the past years had eliminated the voodoo doctors and their weird Friday night ceremonies.

The wild, riotous, uncontrollable element moved to what is now Gallatin Street and in a few years this street became known as "One of a Thousand Murders," where, it was also said, "If you can't dance and won't fight, stand on the side and help drag out the disabled." And if you wanted to fight, why "drop your pistol, pull out your knife, and fight fair."

It was Gallatin Street and not Basin that made New Orleans for many years known "as a fertile field for those who had wild oats to sow," and on Gallatin Street one may sow said oats six days a week, go to church on Sunday, pray for crop failures, and start anew the following Monday. For on this thoroughfare of dilapidated sepulchres, nothing was considered a sin, unless it interfered with Gallatin Street gang.

So rotten became this street that the better element of the city howled long and hard to high heaven and low authorities that those august gentlemen with their politicians' bay windows, whom Gallatin Street said "were as big around as they were high up," eventually withdrew their protection and the wild thoroughfare is no more.

The barrelhouse saloon, father of the present day cabaret, and the barefoot dance halls closed their doors and many of the women moved to the crib houses of Basin Street.

By this time, everything was hunkey-dory on Basin Street, The broads had blossomed out, purchased swell horses and hacks for their heart directors (pimps to the public), hired instructors to teach them how to converse and act in the presence of gentlemen, and wined and dined their friends in the most befitting style. Money came to the harlots like shrimp to a decomposing body in the sea. For the old "district" it was recess time with no dark clouds upon the horizon.

God's portion of the Dear Isle of Orleans was in a deep, sweet day dream. Steam and sailing vessels lined her waterfront. Her banks had almost as much money as the prostitutes. Heart directors hauled the gay dashing blades to the baudy houses at night and their long-green to the banks in the morning. But the black cloud, which always hovers in the offing, burst like a drowned pup upon the "Jewel of the Mississippi Valley" forever destroying her cherished dream of becoming "America's greatest port."

Gold! One of the three things man, sound of mind, will give his all for, was heard upon every street, corner and alley. Gold had been discovered in California and the mad rush to the West Coast began.

Within six months New Orleans became a ghost city. Vacant buildings, business houses, like leper's spots stood alongside one another for block after block. Harlots followed the gold seekers and the money boys ceased coming to the old town to spend their money for new clothes, great food, and a change of love. Old Basin Street, in no time, had all the appearance of an open vault in one of the city's old cemeteries.

From the lack of this regular, rich gravy the old city's financial platter became as bare as a Scotchman's knee, and to this good day she has not been able to make her sweet dream materialize.

As Satan is the product of the hand of God, and entitled to all those who do not profess God, Satan had a just claim upon old Basin Street. Although her financial breath came like an asthmatic's, with his help she survived and kept the emblem of prostitution—a red apple on a white background with one bite missing—flying full mast on its truncheon of sin. To cap a bad climax New Orleans had no faith in the new contraption called "the iron horse."

In 1852 when the rest of the country was served with several thousand miles of railroad, New Orleans did not have a single rail connecting it with anywhere. Placing all faith in water transportation she forever lost the opportunity of becoming America's greatest port.

Out in California the world's greatest boom was in full sway. The early birds struck it rich. The prostitutes struck the early birds with holy bonds of matrimony, settled down, reared families and forgot everything but California.

By 1858 another wild, black cloud was slowly engulfing the nation. War! Civil War! The hardest of all wars upon prostitutes broke in 1861 with all the hatred civilized man is capable of, lifting New Orleans from the depths of despair to unknown heights of a new love. Money! The principal root the tree of sin came again to her like ships under full sail and fair winds, and her ghost-like appearance faded like some women's love.

Red lights again became prominent along Basin Street. So-called cabarets came into existence. Entertainment for soldiers—a place where these tired, weary men could relax and forget the battlefields, cotton patch and old folks back home.

Cabarets! New Orleans once thought the hell-holes of Gallatin Street were about as fetid as man could make them, but the places of business the Civil War brought to Basin Street, made Gallatin look like a church picnic. White Slavery! For a night you want that man's wife; how much will you pay? Bogus marriage certificate, phony priest, rabbis and preachers. Captain, so you need a crew. Dope and smuggling were but a few of the types of business war fetched to Basin Street. Yep! These were hell-holes of New Orleans if such ever existed, and they lasted throughout the war and the period immediately following—Reconstruction Days.

Bacchus, patron saint of the cabaret, served his followers well. Gambling, strong drinks, dope and diseased women, not only almost ruined the health of the city, but sold for fabulous prices to the accompaniment of music drawn from home-made instruments.

One of the first cabarets of importance was the "Union," situated on the downtown lake corner of Iberville and Basin Street. Later, for many years in front of this human maggot house upon a beer keg sat an old Negro man called "Blister Breeches." On a home-made drum with shank bones for drum sticks he pounded out popular tunes of the day. When business was bad he pounded out an old African chant—a tune the Street did not like to hear. For by it the women of the district knew there was no business on Basin Street, and when asked: "What's the tune?" the old Negro would reply, "Dat Boss am de Basin Street Blues."

On Basin Street man and money were plentiful—women scarce. A "yaller gal" (octoroon) above the age of puberty fetched five hundred dollars; a white girl, fair of form and voice, a thousand or more.

From 1860 to 1862 were New Orleans' two richest harvest years. For the old city school was out. Satan, her god, served her well. But dark black clouds again hover near, and like a flash of storm lightning broke, destroying one of the city's four pillars of support—field for those who had wild oats.

General Ben Butler took New Orleans; prostitutes took to parts unknown; bankers took the curtain, and many of God's portion took to garbage cans for a daily substance.

When informed of the harlots' departure, General Butler flew into an uncontrallable rage. It was while the favor of missing women was making his blood boil, he issued an order which decreed prostitutes, particularly the "yaller" gals the city's elite. The women who had fled, upon hearing this, returned, and to the end of the war took most of the Union Soldiers' pay.

General Robert E. Lee passed his sword and peace again returned to the land. Not however for New Orleans. She was invaded by a gang of Washington, D. C., "fancy boys" (carpetbaggers) who with their unlimited power went completely off their rockers, robbing the government like the barrelhouse queen, Ada Hayes' pet coon robbed her patrons. Some of the boys who remained in the old city during the entire war saw their yaller gals being led astray, borrowed the regalia of the Ku Klux Klan and ran the "fancy boys" out of town. 'Long about this time in Washington Senator Summers set up the cry "let's break up them large southern plantations where some men live like sultans with a harem, and give to each Negro man forty acres and a mule." This statement from the Senator really brought the Negroes to New Orleans. Among those who came was Lulu White, an octoroon, and her foster father.

Lulu's dad, very much disappointed, went back to his white folks' plantation in Northern Mississippi, while

Lulu remained and became the consort of a wealthy Mississippi River gambler who in the two hundred block of Basin Street set Lulu up in a four story, thirty-five room place of business which she made famous as the "Hall of Mirrors."

The law of the state permitted one woman to the room. Thirty-five rooms gave Lulu thirty-five girls—all octoroons—seven-eighths white and one-eighth Negro. Her foster father later became her butler and he, as black as an Egypt night, arrayed in his white uniform looked like a fly in a bottle of milk. As one entered the door the old man would greet the visitor with a broad grin and a very polite "May I see the soles on your shoes?" He would examine the heels and soles on your shoes. If not in excellent condition, you did not go in because to get in it was necessary to be well heeled. Floors of the three reception rooms, like the walls and ceiling, were solid pieces of mirror—hence the "Hall of Mirrors."

The most outstanding of this once famous house of prostitution were the two beautiful, life size, marble figures of Eve and the Virgin Mary. Eve stood embracing the serpent with a perfect look of contentment upon her face; the Virgin Mary stood with both feet upon the serpent with a most holy look upon her face. It was in this palace, on the night of January 17, 1894, that jazz music was born, for Basin Street is the birthplace of jazz music.

The boys in the Klan outfit had no more than cleared the town of "fancy boys" when the citizens united and drove Louisiana's Negro Governor out of office, ending the reconstruction days in Louisiana. The democrats took over and financially the city went from bad to worse.

The black sheep of heaven was not, however, to have his work undone, particularly in New Orleans, and the old district held on.

War again came to the rescue of old Basin Street. This time with Spain. The district blossomed out to entertain the soldiers, and likewise became civic-minded, raised a wad of cash and eliminated much of the mud and filth about their homes and streets. The raising of this money, however, proved most unfortunate for the harlots, namely, whenever the politicos desired cash for any purpose they put the screws upon the harlots, heart directors, gamblers, bartenders, hack-drivers and pronto the cash was laid on the barrelhead. Up 'till 1917 this was a favorite source for political revenue.

Blister Breeches

World War I came and old Basin Street fell like a woman's breast, never to rise again. The fight the ladies had started had at last borne good fruit. Some, however, say it was not the ladies or the church but the good roads, automobiles on the easy payment plan, hip-pocket flask and the charitable amateur that put old Basin Street out of business.

The writer, however, is of the opinion it was the long, constant, united effort of both the church and the ladies, coupled with placing the right kind of men in public office, which eventually led to the downfall of this once infamous thoroughfare—Old Basin Street. "Her sins be forgiven for she hath loved much."

Quadroon Ballroom

The Quadroon Ballroom, situated on Orleans near Royal street, is the only building in the city to have completely changed from one of rottenness to one of purity. Also the only one when mentioned in the presence of native historians that will cause these gentlemen to place a finger to the mouth and whisper "sh-sh." For in the early activities of the Ballroom, should one care to delve deeper, the true cause of the Civil War would be found—yellow women. Hence among said historians the Quadroon Ballroom, is seldom if ever mentioned.

The building, a two-story, box-like structure, erected in 1820, housed a private cabaret for after theatre parties, which served only the exclusive patrons from the old Theatre d'Orleans. Here theatre goers would gather after a performance for a drink or two, a bite to eat, and to make what now a high school boy would call "whoopee".

One cold wet winter night in 1824, a wild party got too wild. Fire broke out, doing considerable damage to the second floor, and leaving the building an eye sore and a natural home for rats until 1826, when the State of Louisiana leased the building, renovated and converted it into a legislative hall. Here until 1828 the state's Senators and Representatives met, and passed, repealed, swapped and violated laws. By the end of the second year the people had tired of their law makers' capers, blamed their actions on the past atmosphere of the building, and moved these pretentious gentlemen to other quarters.

At this time several, gay dashing blades, each with bank accounts equal in length to Jacob's ladder, and a following of "yaller gals" as long as a prophet's dream got an idea—A Quadroon Ballroom.

Leaving the outside of the building as it was—ugly and forlorn—they expended considerable time and money upon the inside, particularly the dance floor and interior decorations.

Because of the large sum of money spent to aid and delight dancing feet, it is still the nation's finest dance floor. It consists of three layers of hand-sawed cypress laid crosswise, and topped with a layer of hard finished oak.

At one end was the bandstand, boarded up some three feet above the platform with heavy oak timbers. This furnished the negro musicians with ample protection from wild or well directed shots often fired by some "blade" who had managed to smuggle in a gun, and who had imbibed at least one too many "blue-eyed tigers".

The ceiling, extremely high, was well decorated with huge paintings which were supposed to excite certain emotions. Neatly arranged around the walls were two rows of comfortable chairs, chained to the floor—this precaution saved many a skull from being fractured. At a convenient distance from the front row of chairs ran a heavy oak railing, dividing the spectators from the dancers. Should one stray alone on the floor, he was immediately, but politely asked to leave. The second time he was ejected by two immense, meaty bouncers.

To gain entrance to this famous Ballroom it was necessary to be the possessor of at least one "yaller gal." Later, however, this system was abolished in favor of one of introduction. By the time the Texas revolution was under way a "dam Yankee" could get in with out knowing a native soul. Having no admission fee, the Ballroom was completely supported by favors and by the revenue from the drinks sold.

Upon entering, the first person encountered was the negro butler, arrayed in many colors. He looked like the rainbow might look if ever struck by lightning. It has been said "it was from reading about this negro butler that the late U. S. Senator, Huey P. Long got the idea for his personal color scheme."

When the butler had relieved the guest of his hat, the visitor passed on to where he met a white man of vast proportions. This gentleman, attired in evening clothes, relieved him of all deadly weapons. If a bit doubtful the big fellow had the legal right to frisk the guest's person for hidden guns, knives, etc. The next stop was the bar, which was usually lined three deep with men of all ages and means. Yellow women moved among them like a giant python, silent, oily and with more poison upon their tongues than could be found in a bushel of Missouri rattle-snakes. Some of the gentlemen, already weak from age and liquor could hardly support the yellow woman hanging upon his arm.

The favorite drink was the "blue-eyed tiger." Others in favor were the "bark peeler", Snapping turtle", and the "Alligator gargle". None was by no means overlooked. The yellow women, realizing they could make no money when drunk drank tea in their concoctions, and when possible emptied their drinks upon the floor. Any two of these drinks would afford sufficient courage to stare at any man's "yaller gal", and make his way with the aid of the sturdy oak banister on the winding Spanish stairway, to the second floor where the dancers' feet rattled the building's timbers.

If the drinks had not robbed the mind of all reasoning power one would search among the crowd for an unattached yellow woman, preferably an octoroon (seven-eighths white and one-eighth negro." These women known as "blondes" were very much sought after. For as the men about town said: "Blondes are always preferable because they soiled so quickly." If a fellow looked like he might be somebody he did not have long to wait. Gentlemen alone in the Quadroon Ballroom did not remain long without a *roonish* friend.

It was the custom when once coralled to purchase the new found friend a drink. This meant returning to the bar and then to the cobble-stoned courtyard for later arrangements, and then again to the dance for as many sets as one could go.

If a man, danced unto the wee hours of the morn' without stepping upon some "yaller gal's" corns, he indeed was most fortunate. For such was a crime and sufficient cause for a challenge to a duel, arrangements for which would be made before daylight. Should a "dam Yankee" be challenged to a duel, he would shout "I don't fight duels, I hire lawyers!" But to the young New Orleans gallant it was different. His cry was "meet me in St. Anthony's Garden at sun rise with your choice of weapons!"

The rising sun's first rays barely had time to pierce the darkness of the night when the duelists and their seconds gathered in St. Anthony's Garden (at the rear of the St. Louis Cathedral) where some second could be heard to say, "It's pistols for two. Coffee for one."

The garden" was the site of many duels. Most of them were fought over the city's fascinating yellow women . The priests of the Cathedral eventually became tired of this early morning pistol serenade and asked these gentlemen if they could not find some other place to duel. The dueling oaks in City Park then became the meeting place for exponents of the *Code duello.*

The gory gaiety of the Quadroon Ballroom is no more. Time, custom and tide of events has changed its once rottenness into a state of purity. For today the building houses the Sisters of the Holy Family, an order of negro nuns, who conduct a parochial school for children of their race.

Pakenham Ruins

Two and three-quarter miles south of the city of New Orleans stands what today is commonly called Pakenham Ruins. The ruins were originally the home of De La Ronde, a Spanish nobleman, cousin of Charles II, King of Spain and a disappointed lover of Catherine the Great, Empress of Russia. The Don, greatly embittered by Catherine's sudden termination of his love making, decided to exile himself in the New World. He went to Charles III and received a grant of land in what is now St. Bernard parish or county.

The Don arrived in New Orleans two days before the great fire of Good Friday, 1788. The conflagration had so confounded the people the Don decided to build immediately, and in this manner give help in the form of employment. The kind of material his house should be built of the fire decided for him. The city had on hand about half the amount of brick needed. They were large and cumbersome and none were perfect in shape. The Don, not wishing to wait for brick to come from Spain, made a search of the countryside for a suitable clay. It was found at what is now Slidell, and there the state's first bricks were manufactured. The Don instructed that the brick be made in size half that of the Spanish brick.

In viewing the ruins today one can easily see the brick in the first story are much larger than those of the second. The home was a box-like structure with sixteen rooms. The first floor a foot and a half above ground, and made of flagstones. There was a full length veranda on both the east and west sides. Each window had a small balcony with raillings of grille. The roof was steep and covered with tile shingles. The building, for twenty feet on all sides, was terraced. The home was erected on a slight ridge a quarter of a mile from the river, and true to an ancient Catholic custom, it faced east.

In those days there were no roads; transportation was by water, therefore the Don built a wide shell road from the home to the river. Each side of the lane was lined with young oak trees.

Catherine, Empress of Russia, had once told the Don that she had been loved by four hundred men, and fifty-two of them were royalty, the Don in honor of these fifty-two royal lovers set out a tree for each. The line of oaks extended from the home to the river, twenty-six on one side and twenty-five on the other. As the Don considered himself the most outstanding lover, the tree which represented him must be outstanding and it is, as one can see today.

The Oak Grove is considered one of the country's finest and is known locally as the Cathedral of Oaks. General Pakenham, the English Commander during the Battle of Orleans, made these ruins his headquarters. He was mortally wounded on the field of battle January 8, 1815, and was carried to the ruins, where he died in the afternoon.

The ruins today is private property. However, to afford it some protection, it is under the control of the

Colonial Dames residents of Louisiana. It is today the property of the Southern railroad. Some time in the near future both the grove of oaks and the ruins will be incorporated in the proposed Jackson National Park, which is to be constructed out of the Battlefields of New Orleans.

Marie le Veau

Voodooism is a form of ophiolatry, a Negro religion originating in Africa. And as a religious faith, Voodooism entered the white race with the Israelites while they were in bondage to the Egyptians, as slaves picking cotton in the Pharaoh's fields. For this reason it has been said, "God raised Moses to deliver his people from man's most accursed curse — Voodooism." From the Israelites it spread to the Chaldeans, Druids and Magi. Greeks were the first to test Voodooism for truth—and they proved it a fraud.

The early Christian Church saw in Voodooism a powerful weapon, adopted it, changed the ritual and called it "Witchcraft." This new faith, witchcraft, in the hands of so-called civilized man soon proved to be a far greater curse than Voodooism. For centuries the church founded upon the Rock carried campaigns of murder, defloration, arson and other rapacious acts in its name. Witchcraft fastened itself upon the once solid Rock to such an extent it crushed it into more than five hundred pieces.

One bit of fragment, Wesley by name declared that to give up witchcraft was to give up the Bible.

Another fragment, Presbyterian, hired professional witch hunters and appointed two eminent ministers to travel with them. Their duty was to tour the English countryside and stick pins into old women to determine whether or not they were witches. All whom these three —and whom the church said were "holy men"—found guilty, were immediately executed.

The above however, is water long since passed under the bridge. Modern science is rapidly proving that superstition can be and is being eliminated from the hearts of men. However, Voodooism in New Orleans is still worthy of note. Not only is it believed in, but practised by people one would ordinarily think would know better than to place faith in such things.

One of the most famous great open Voodoo ceremonies of the Western world was staged by Marie le Veau.

Upon a throne of living reptiles, Marie le Veau's amber-skinned body, arrayed in a short skirt of fig leaves, swayed like the hanging reptiles draping her make-shift throne. Her round, firm breast, cause of many a duel—rose and fell in slow, even, tantalizing rhythm. Her arms were limp and gently swaying. Her dainty feet rested upon the back of a huge alligator with mouth propped open and suffering the tortures of Hades.

With head bent back Marie le Veau gazed, her large brown eyes just beyond the striking reptiles, whose poisonous fangs came within inches of her enchanting face.

The hour was late. Neither moon or stars were shining. Large gourds cut to resemble grotesque faces cast their pale yellow light upon the thousand or more Negroes gathered before her throne in Congo Square. As they kneeled, bowed and perspired their weird, mournful chant echoed and re-echoed against the swamp on the west and the river on the east, filling the white citizenry of New Orleans with an uncanny feeling.

Somewhere in the Old French Quarter, a clock tolled the hour of midnight. The Negroes came to their feet in time to see the spirit of Marie le Veau, in the form of a white bird take wing into the distant ocean of darkness for its rendezvous with the great Zombi. Her spirit had barely departed when Marie began to groan as in terrible pain. The Negroes believing an evil spirit was attempting to possess the heart of their queen, waved their arms, jumped and shouted until Marie raised her right hand and the turmoil ceased as if by magic.

Overhead the Negroes, heard a wild rushing noise. Looking up they beheld three great black birds with yellow tipped wings circling madly above their heads, then rising to disappear into the black depth of the night.

As the Negroes held their breath, between Marie's right arm and body there came a nine foot African python. Its gorgeous colored skin, recently oiled, radiated the flickering yellow light like an immense cluster of diamonds, as it moved rather uncertainly forward.

Unnoticed, Marie directed the reptile's course around her trim waist until its large, flat, cold and ugly head lay snugly between her warm breasts. The long forked tongue caressed her chin a time or two and then relaxed, allowing its coil to rest upon her beautifully formed hips. Marie gave vent to a long sigh and again the Negroes shouted and jumped with joy, for their queen protected by the giant reptile could not now be possessed by an evil spirit.

Before her throne of dry, cypress tree limbs, coated with powdered white shell, decorated with dead moss and palm fronds, stood the altar. Twelve feet in length, three feet wide. It was floored with poles tied together of strips of willow tree bark, topped with grass and dirt. Facing east in the center of the altar was a medium sized stuffed alligator with mouth propped open. Into the open jaws the Negroes trembling with fear cast their free will offerings. To the right of the alligator was a stuffed snake. To the left a small plant, the Tree of Life. Beneath the plant was a small doll like image of a woman representing the weakness of man. A shelf a foot high and equally as wide extended the full length of the altar. In the center of the shelf stood the ancient mystic Abyssinian number FIVE. Along the shelf, left to right were five flat mud cakes piled one upon the other representing the five continents; five dry gourds of water representing the five oceans; five piles of dirt representing the five soils; five mud cups representing the five original poisons, and the square and compass the two tools the great Zombi used in dividing the earth from the waters and with which he used to extract the rib from man to create woman and to make each life true to its specie.

Along the altar the Negroes placed their gifts; sacks of corn, sides of meat, onions, potatoes, fowls—live and cooked—preserves, cakes, pies, jars of honey, boiled crayfish, thistle salad, praline candy, fresh fruit and many other delicacies. The altar piled high and no more in sight. Marie clapped her hands and the Negroes looked up and saw her with five birds in her left hand, four bluejays and a red bird. The red bird she sent to the land of evil spirits to tell the Devil that his services for the night were not needed. He might, however, for a short while send a spirit to sell his wicked charms to the people. The four jays she sent to the four corners of the earth to warn the keepers of these corners an evil spirit would be abroad in the land for some time during the night. The jays had no more than departed when from somewhere in the dismal swamp, west of Congo Square came the rat-a-ta-tat of an African drum. A nerve racking noise which chilled and rechilled the white citizen's blood.

A thousand or more Negroes with hearts overflowing with hate for their white masters; Union soldiers not allowed within two blocks of where these Negroes were gathered; General Ben Butler soaked in wine, smelling like a crate of sour grapes and two, teen-age octoroon girls pouring the General more wine, would chill the blood of any unarmed white person.

To this hellish sound all New Orleans listened. The Negroes understanding its meaning, also listened with eagerness. It told them they were to be visited by an evil spirit who would offer for sale the devil's finest and quick acting charms.

The drum beats ceased as abruptly as they began. The Negroes relaxed and beheld before the altar, a tall, slim cowled figure arrayed in black. "An evil spirit" they whispered, as their blood chilled and rechilled. Marie raised an arm and the Negroes' heathen blood came back to normal.

The cowled figure looked up at Marie. She smiled and it turned towards the Negroes. In a voice sounding like low, distant thunder it said, "Listen! The Deb'l, he say fo' me to tell yo' dis. All yo' what got muder, hate, envy, arson, stealing, lying, rape, jealousy, distrust, vanity or any other kind ob pisen in yo' hearts, meet me on de St. Ann street side of de square and get fo yo'self de kind ob charm yo' needs to do de wurk yo' wonts done. Kase de time am short. 'Av yo' money ready. De Deb'i, he don't do nuffen but de barrel head business."

Again the drum beats split the night cutting short whatever else the cowled figure might have said. As the Negroes listened in stupified wonder, their blood chilling, the cowled figure ducked under the altar, grabbing a half-filled grain sack, swung it over his shoulder and departed for the forementioned side of the Square. Quickly, a previously placed barrel was rolled out, stood on end, over which was cast a black goat hide, and there the figure stood, waiting for the drum to end its hated beat. No more than it did, the Negroes rushed over and for thirty minutes this evil spirit did a black market business.

Young girls purchased all sorts of powder. Some to fetch a man, another kind to drive one away; powder to take kinks out of their hair; to thin the lips; to make both legs alike; to make their white madam sick that she would have no more babies; and that the silverware would disappear.

Young men purchased powder for practically the same purposes as did the girls.

Older women bought charms, fish scales to keep white folk's company away; dry worms to make visitors ill and go home; small boxes of roaches to liberate in the house whereby there would be less clothes to wash and horsehair rings to drive pediculi from the heads of their own children to those of week-end guests.

Older men spent their money buying powder which would bring them young women; small white pebbles to place in the harness to make mules ill; shells to make it rain when the cotton needed hoeing; dry boll-weevils to make the cotton easy to pick and many other kinds of charms for various purposes.

The rat-a-tat-tat of the far distant drum ended the evil spirit's business and the Negroes like frightened sheep ran to the throne of Marie, who with the old familiar wave of the hand ended the horrible noise and the Negroes spread out some.

In good English, Marie announced: "The spirit of the great Zombi will soon be with us. And to please him, the girls are going to do his favorite dance—the Congo or Bamboula."

Two giant Negroes with large, heavy poles came forward and pushed the throng back, shouting, "Make room for the dancers!"

Out of the dark, bounded twelve nude, beautiful, amber-skinned octoroon girls arrayed only with two palmetto fronds carried in each hand, one in front and the other to the rear. The young men shouted with joy. Old men cursed their age. The young girls prayed to the great Zombi to be Congo dancers, and the older women beat their husbands with whatever they could lay hands upon.

The dance imitated the movements of the African python both on the ground and among the trees for some twenty minutes. The dancers with one eye on the crowd and the other upon Marie, saw her soft hands come together and they broke through the circle the Negroes had formed to make a get-a-way, or be caught by some fleet-footed male. The spectators jumped and shouted with joy and the white citizens again felt their blood chill. Marie let them shout until they fell from sheer exhaustion.

There was a short breathing space, then she called them nearer to the throne. In a quiet voice she told them "the great Zombi has sent a spirit man who has charms which will bring us good luck."

A short, round, plump figure arrayed in white appeared and spread along the altar the great Zombi's stock —bones from a white man's grave to keep the evil spirits away; dry crayfish claws filled with gray powder to quicken love, heal the sick and act in various other ways.

The Negroes however, had spent their money with the evil spirit and so the Great Zombi's charms went begging.

Observing they had no more money, Marie dismissed them with the reminder never to forget the 19th day of June and to celebrate it with a Voodoo ceremony in honor of Abraham Lincoln, Emancipator of the Negroes.

The Negroes departed and Marie had a cart haul away the gifts upon which her aids would wax fat for many weeks.

The sun was just beginning to knife the darkness in the east when Marie reached her home on Dumaine Street where she was very much surprised to learn the two "yaller" gals whom she sent with four bottles of wine to entertain General Butler and gain his consent to have the meeting, as yet had not returned. But knowing Butler's fondness for wine and "yaller" gals she dismissed all concern and retired for a much needed rest.

The yellow girls had executed their missions very well. They wined, dined and danced with Butler until he issued the order which permitted Marie to hold her Voodoo ceremony. By noon of the third day, Butler sobered to the extent he would see visitors, had several leading citizens call upon him. They remonstrated with him for permitting the beautiful Marie le Veau to practise her black art.

Referring to Marie as beautiful, automatically put them out of his office. As soon as they were gone, Butler dispatched soldiers to fetch Marie to see him.

General Butler, like other white men who had the opportunity to be alone with Marie le Veau lost all sense of reasoning, in the atmosphere where she radiated allure, enchantment and tantalizing delight. And when she answered Butler with a "no" he saw red. Flying into an uncontrollable rage, he outlawed her activities, confiscaing everything she possessed.

Marie with a bowed head and broken heart, left Butler's office never again to regain her former power or self-confidence. A year later, she died and was buried by friends in a St. Louis cemetery.

Her unmarked grave today is a shrine for thousands who believe in spirits and voodooism. They go to the grave and make the sign of the cross upon it and pray for favors. This is particularly true during the race horse season.

To reach her grave, enter the Iberville street gate of St. Louis cemetery, Number Two. Turn right, and the end of the wall-vault, second from the top, many people believe to be her grave.

This was Marie le Veau's last ceremony, January 27, 1862. Louisiana seceded from the Union. And the States withdrawal outlawed all forms of Voodooism and fortune telling which ended Marie's activities in black art. May 2, 1862, General Benjamin E. Butler, took over New Orleans and overrode all state laws, and by so doing, gained the name of "Beast Butler."

Marie le Veau

Marie learned the General's weakness by studying his behavior and then the desire swept her to hold one more Voodoo ceremony; that the Negroes might honor Abraham Lincoln for his efforts in their behalf, and to implore the great Zombi to fight upon the side of Lincoln.

To have any sort of meeting, it was necessary to have a permit from General Butler. Having discovered the General's soft spot, she sent with a bottle of fine, French wine under each arm, two, young, fair octoroon girls to gain Butler's permission.

Within a few hours after the girls departed Marie's home, two Union soldiers knocked upon her alley gate with the permit and the following night, Marie le Veau staged the western world's last greatest open Voodoo ceremony.

Voodooism in Plaquemines Parish

Voodooism, as practiced in Plaquemines Parish was utterly different and not connected with the rites practiced in New Orleans.

Voodooism in Plaquemines Parish was a fetish religion. Worshiping idols, worshipers, like their savage ancestors of a thousand years ago believed the images became living beings which could see, hear, understand, and all who had faith would have their favors granted.

Voodooism in New Orleans was but a crude form of magic, presided over by a human being called a king or queen who had been blessed by a great Zombi with powers to endow an object with magical properties.

The short distance between the two communities will no doubt cause one to ask: "Why such a wide difference in theory and practice between two groups of Negroes addicted to voodooism?" For a better understanding it might be in order to know something of the early settlers of Plaquemines Parish.

Bordering upon the Gulf of Mexico that parish (county), a bit south of New Orleans, is mostly swamp and marsh land. Until the last few years the only form of transportation was by water.

In the year 1479 two events happened in Spain, both having a direct bearing upon our problem. The first was the marriage of Isabella, Infanta of Castile, and Prince Ferdinand of Aragon. The prince upon becoming Ferdinand the Fifth, King of Spain, was not long in showing the strength of his hand. One of his first official acts and the second event affecting our story was to banish the Moors from the land. This caused many a Castilian Spaniard to howl to high heaven. With the echo of their cries constantly in his ear, and upon the suggestion of Cortez, a Spanish national legislator, egged on by the Inquisition, Ferdinand banished many prominent Castilians to the Canary Islands. As these exiles came from the same part of Spain as Isabella, Ferdinand permitted them to take along much of their wealth and personal property.

The Canary Islands were bare of the things these cultured and aristocratic Spaniards had been accustomed to. They liked gardens, architecture, statuary and art. They petitioned Ferdinand for permission to bring in Greek marble workers, painters and Ethiopian Negroes for slave labor. They claimed the Congo Negro lacked the mental capacity for quick learning. Their slaves came from Eastern Africa and not from the Guinea Coast.

In 1762, France ceded Louisiana to Spain. It was not, however, until 1766 that the Louisiana French learned of this transfer. They objected and two years later revolted and drove the Spanish out of New Orleans. The following summer (1769) the King of Spain dispatched to

Louisiana two thousand soldiers under the command of one Don O'Reilly, an Irishman who had been made a general in the Spanish army.

The general's method of shooting first and questioning later, quickly ended the revolt, but gained for himself the title of "Bloody O'Reilly."

This rebellion determined the King of Spain to populate Louisiana with true Spaniards, some of Spain's best blood. For this purpose he turned to the exiles of the Canary Islands. To these people he offered freedom, large grants of land in Louisiana, and transportation if they would make this section of the new world their home.

Many accepted the King's offer. From crude maps they were granted large tracts of land. They were in complete ignorance of the fact their land was but a country of swamp, mud, alligators, reptiles and mosquitoes, inhabited by Congo Negroes and a few Frenchmen who wanted nothing more than to hunt, fish, trap and fraternize with the aboriginal Indian.

Much disappointed the Castilians with their Negroes made the best of a bad situation. They established what is now called "Plaquemines Parish." Incidentally this is one of the few spots on the globe where—so to speak—a living will fall into one's mouth. Other than its social customs which are of old Spain—clanish and seclusive—it's a poor man's paradise. Although its population today is of many bloods—pure and mixed—there are no true Cajuns or Creoles to be found there.

Their Negroes, descendants of the Ethiopians fetched to the Canary Islands, were like their ancestors, believers in images, not magic. For the want of an image they made one from mud, dry moss and colored it a pearl gray with river sand. Illustration, on last page will give some idea of its size.

Having no particular medicine man they were presided over by a middle-aged Negro, whom the Negroes believed had the power of the "evil eye." This type of Negro later became a fixture on all southern plantations. He did no work of any kind, wore his master's best cast-off clothing, ate the best of food, and was of considerable importance in his white-folks household. This led the Negroes to believe he had the power over the "evil eye." What, however, they did not know was that his ability to do this came through the white children on the plantation.

On summer evenings, not far from the house, beneath a tree this rascal could be found entertaining the white children with his wild, weird tales of animals, beasts, fish, fowls and how they lived and fought, and the might and power of the Ethiopian witch doctor. His fertile brain, never tiring or failing to interest the children, was the source of his good fortune, and his success had no connection with the "evil eye." Whenever he became involved in any kind of difficulty, regardless of its nature, the children came to his rescue, and of course he always escaped punishment. Thus by his wits the man who would have become a witch doctor in his native haunts overcame circumstances and seemed to obtain almost supernatural power. It was therefore natural, when the Negroes of Plaquemines decided to have a god of their own, to turn to the local plantation charlatan for leadership. Under his supervision, during their leisure time, they built their mud figure.

When possible the figure was placed in the center of a circle three hundred feet in diameter, on a ridge-like elevation, deep in the swamp. In the dead of the night, on the first full moon of each month the Negroes would hold their regular monthly meeting.

Several hours before the members of the cult gathered for their ceremonies our "rascal friend" would collect and cut into small pieces, three bushel-baskets of leaves from the Zambezian castor plant. He then broadcasted the leaves until the entire circle was covered. The odor from these leaves kept away such insects as mosquitoes, nats, spiders and so on. Our voodoo leader was wise enough to give the image the credit and not himself for the absence of mosquitoes. Consequently he ruled the Negroes with logic that was as real as their mud god.

Around this mud figure, on a carpet of cut leaves, led by the voodoo charlatan the Negroes would sing, shout and dance, and ask their god for favors. Working themselves into a state of high emotion they would often swear they could see the image's lips move in answer to their questions.

Into the late hours of the morning they would continue these fetish revels until exhausted. They were never molested by the white man, for to witness this fantastic orgy no white person would brave the swamp at night.

Looking upon their religious activities as a harmless relaxation, the Spaniards, did not bother the Negroes. To them it was noticeable that for days afterwards the Negroes who attended these meetings were in good spirits. And any southerner will tell you that the best Negro is one in "high spirits."

The Castilian Spaniards, by their silence gave their approval to the Negro's voodoo activities. This form of primitive fetichism spread rapidly among the Negroes living in the great swamp section of the deep South. Even today such voodoo rites are conducted in remote places but in the deepest secrecy. If the modern devotees of Plaquemines voodooism possess a mud god they conceal its whereabouts. Nobody knows where one may be seen.

Paul Tulane

Paul Tulane, founder of the great university in New Orleans that bears his name, was a Frenchman, Roman Catholic, and a native of Princeton, New Jersey.

Tulane, due to his family's financial condition, left school at the early age of fifteen. A year later, in company with a cousin, he made a tour of the United States. Because of Tulane's curiosity to see a pirate, they came to New Orleans to see Jean Lafitte, the pirate. At that time Lafitte was conducting a blacksmith shop. Dirty, shirtless, and barefooted, with his pants legs cut off at the knees, Lafitte stood at the forge when Tulane and his companion entered the shop. Tulane, who acted as spokesman, asked to see Mr. Lafitte, the pirate.

Lafitte looked up, smiled, and answered, "I am Lafitte, but I am no pirate." Tulane thanked him and left the shop greatly disappointed.

More to himself than to his cousin, he muttered, "That cannot be Lafitte the Pirate from Barataria."

Tulane inquired of many prominent people if that man in the blacksmith shop was Lafitte, the pirate. Finally, he became convinced that this was Lafitte and visited with him for hours every day during his stay in New Orleans. Tulane took a great liking for Lafitte and likewise Lafitte for him.

Just before leaving New Orleans, Tulane told Lafitte that when he became of age he would like to come back to New Orleans and work for him, because he, too, wanted to learn the art of working in iron. Lafitte advised Tulane that he would not be in New Orleans upon his return. He also told him that should he come back and still desire to be an iron worker, to go across the river and ask for a man named John McDonogh and he would further advise him what to do.

Paul Tulane, true to his word, returned to New Orleans the same year he became of age. He immediately sought John McDonogh and, when McDonogh was convinced of his identity, he informed Tulane that Lafitte had left two thousand dollars in gold in his care for him. With this money he was to enter the iron business under the supervision of John McDonogh. Tulane gladly accepted these conditions. McDonogh did not immediately turn the money over to Tulane, but placed it in a mercantile business and within a few years Tulane became the firm's head.

A strong and lasting friendship sprang up between these two; Tulane had such high esteem for McDonogh that he renounced his religion for that of his friend, and became a Presbyterian.

Here we leave Paul Tulane and turn back the pages of history to about 1808, at which time there was an uprising of the Mulatto Negroes on the Isle of St. Domingo. Every white person who did not escape was murdered. This wholesale slaughter of whites history refers to as the Yellow Massacre of the Isle of St. Domingo. The black Negro having no part in this uprising was also massacred.

While this massacre was taking place, Dominique You, the right hand man of Jean Lafitte, was in the Caribbean sea contacting all pirates, spreading the information that loot could be disposed of at Barataria for a fair price and with all safety. By chance he crossed the path of one of the ships which fled St. Domingo with refugees bound for Mexico. Dominique first hailed her to halt; this was ignored. He then placed a well-aimed shot across her bow; this, too, was ignored. He next fired a shot which tore away the main mast. With a few men,

Dominique boarded the ship, and found a crew of thirty-odd drunken mulatto Negroes, brandishing swords, knives, whiskey bottles and marlin pins. As Dominique and his men came over the side of the ship, the crew charged. It was not long, however, before Dominique had the situation in hand. The crew was lined against the ship's rail and Dominique searched the ship. Aboard he found a hysterical white girl lying in a bunk. Dominique took the white woman aboard his ship and sailed for Barataria.

In 1814, when the United States government destroyed Barataria and dispersed its people, Miss McCarty, the girl rescued by You, came to New Orleans, where later she married and became Madame Lalaurie. McDonogh, through his connection with Jean Lafitte, became her advisor, and through him she met his protegé, Paul Tulane who fell madly in love with her. Tulane thereafter spent much of his time in her presence. Although Madame Lalaurie often said she did not love her husband, she would not leave him. Even this did not stop Tulane from making love to her. Accordingly, he made a vow that if he could not wed Madame Lalaurie he would wed no other woman.

The night her home caught fire, Paul Tulane had accompanied her to the French Opera House. When notified her home was afire and people were breaking in, she confessed to Tulane her cruel treatment of her Mulatto Negroes. Although Tulane had heard this accusation of cruelty against her, he took no stock in it.

In order to escape the angry crowd, Tulane arranged for her to go to Mandeville, Louisiana, for a few days, and later to the McDonogh plantation. Here she remained in seclusion until Tulane could secure passage to France for her.

For twenty-four years Tulane waited in New Orleans for her promised return. In 1858, he received word that Madame Lalaurie had died in France a raving maniac.

Broken hearted, Tulane quietly disposed of all his Louisiana possessions. Before quitting the state for good, Tulane followed in the footsteps of the man who had made him wealthy, John McDonogh. He, too, gave and planned to give more for the education of Louisiana's youth. John McDonogh gave that his name might not be forgotten; Tulane gave in the honor and memory of the only woman he ever loved. He confided to a few close friends that he would like the school he endowed to be given the name Lalaurie. These friends finally persuaded him that the name of Lalaurie would be detrimental to the university. Upon the suggestion of these friends the university bears his name. Tulane did insist that as long as the university bears his name, its spiritual faith must be Presbyterian, and its presidents preferably Masons.

And as all good stories go, Tulane died a wealthy bachelor, leaving to America a wonderful institution of learning founded on pirate gold and a man's love for a cold, cruel-hearted, insane woman.

New Orleans in 1861

In 1861 we find New Orleans in good shape financially. Her river trade was at its best, her foreign trade growing. Her merchants rubbed their hands together in deep satisfaction, the Negroes along the riverfront were singing merrily. The prostitutes purchased land a block west of the French Quarter and founded New Orleans notorious red light districts. There they built elaborate homes with walls and floors of mirrors, and scoured the South for young beautiful yellow girls. Many white men have made small fortunes keeping these houses supplied with such girls, for in this life a girl ages quickly. At twenty she is considered an old woman.

Money was plentiful, prices high, still New Orleans felt secure to the extent that her people refused to comment on the black talk. Although Abraham Lincoln was elected on a Republican ticket, was he not Democratic at heart? So strong was their belief in this the natives claimed that with Lincoln as president there would be no civil war.

As to how Lincoln felt upon the question of slavery, New Orleans knew. Tradition tells us in 1831 young Lincoln came down the Mississippi river on a flatboat. Due to the horrible stories he had heard of New Orleans' riverfront, Lincoln and his party chose the west bank of the river to land. Here the slaves of John McDonogh, a wealthy plantation owner and money lender, came to the river. Lincoln slept on the flatboat with two others of the party. A few nights after his arrival Lincoln was awakened by a noise. Taking a club he chased the prowlers into the river. The following morning Lincoln set out to learn who his callers of the previous night were, and discovered they were Negroes and the property of John McDonogh. Lincoln reported the incident to McDonogh, who wanted to whip the Negroes. To this Lincoln would not listen and suggested that they be made to work all day on an empty stomach. This, he believed would be better punishment and would not hurt them as he had worked many days without food.

During the course of conversation, McDonogh asked Lincoln if he had ever seen Negroes sold at public auction. When he answered in the negative, McDonogh invited him to attend a sale in the afternoon at 628 Royal street. Among the Negroes to be sold, McDonogh had a yellow girl about sixteen years of age. She was placed upon the block and the auctioneer eulogized her qualities of beauty, form, etc. The sale much slower than McDonogh thought it should be. To make the sale more interesting, McDonogh stepped up to the block and jerked the girl's dress off, leaving her nude and crying.

Lincoln, as the story goes, gritted his teeth and with a well directed blow floored McDonogh, walked out of the auction room and never again returned to New Orleans.

Accordingly, it is said, New Orleans knew how Lincoln felt about slavery, yet believed that with him as their leader there would be no civil war. So strong was this belief, plans were made for the celebration of his inauguration. Money for parades and other entertainments, as usual, was furnished by gamblers, saloon keepers, bartenders, hack drivers, prostitutes and pimps.

Back of town, in the old Congo Square, a beautiful yellow girl and voodoo queen, was holding a riotous voodoo ceremony in honor of Lincoln. Indians, Negroes, half-breeds, and the poor whites were eating, drinking and shouting, "Long live Honest Abe!" while the yellow girls did the Bamboula dance. Because of the importance of the occasion, these girls danced nude except for the palmetto frond they carried in each hand. Marie le Veau, on her throne of fig leaves (fig leaves is the emblem of purity in voodooism), canopied with palmetto fronds dyed various colors. She clothed in a silk loin cloth, had around her nude waist an entwined ten-foot snake— the South American boa constrictor, alive, but in a stuper. Her giant black Negro body guard, Okie Pokie, who was always near, had for two hours preceding the ceremony, burned the leaves of the marahuana plant in the reptile's cage, deadening its powers of constriction. The people, wild in their enthusiasm, danced like madmen around her, while she prophesied that 1861 was going to be a great year. Abraham Lincoln would be a friend to white as well as the black, and if all was left to him there would be no war.

These ignorant people believed that beautiful yellow witch despite the fact that Louisiana had already seceded from the Union, the governor of Alabama had seized the federal arsenal at Mount Vernon near Mobile, and the governor of Georgia had seized the forts of Pulaski and Jackson near Savannah. How wrong the voodoo queen and the people of New Orleans were, accepted history tells us.

Civil war came. Abraham Lincoln freed the Negroes and his Union army shot down the poor whites. New Orleans declared that she would have no part in the impending war as she was Southern only in location and had become the property of the United States through no choice of her own. She was in existence when those Yankee states were British colonies; she would join with the state of Louisiana and set up an independent government. In accordance with this doctrine, she joined the state of Louisiana in choosing a flag, hoisted it to the world as an independent state and prepared herself for big business in the role of the banker.

The City Care Forgot

In the spring of 1861 General Beauregard took Fort Sumpter, President Lincoln called for volunteers and the war between the states was on. On for what? asked many New Orleans people. For what are they fighting and what is to be gained? It cannot be war because of the Negroes! there must be some other cause. Whatever the cause we will have no part in it. This is what one class thought. Another class, the bankers, brokers and importers, thought otherwise, for they could see vast fortunes to be made out of war. All that was necessary was for New Orleans to remain neutral and they could reap the harvest greed had sown.

Finance ruled then as it does today. Events turned as the latter class desired and New Orleans became the world's busiest port. Men, old and young, came to New Orleans from all directions to enlist in the army. Most of these men had some money, but spent it with the yellow women back of town before visiting the recruiting office. Soon after their enlistment, many of these men, because of their visits back of town, became unfit for military service. As a result they were discharged and became a burden to the Confederate cause. Many of these men who were unable to work drifted back to New Orleans and revived the old business of river piracy.

If business ever hummed on the New Orleans riverfront, it did in late 1861 and early 1862. Ships flying flags of all nations could be seen, eight or ten abreast, taking on and discharging cargoes. As soon as one ship with a completed cargo was pushed out into the river, marlin and belaying pins started flying as crews of nearby ships fought for her berth. At that time New Orleans did not have the modern docks she has today. Her wharves were made of logs loosely fitted. Merchandise was piled high and covered with tarpaulin.

Brokers, buyers, longshoremen and peddlers all moved in a hurry. One never asked the other what he was doing. Petty thieving thrived, police in their efforts to stop it only made bad matters worse. The wise ones ceased carting stolen merchandise, claimed ownership and sold it on the wharf. The same batch of goods was often sold by the same party more than once. The Confederacy paid for a cargo several times before it ever left the waterfront. Meat and flour became wormy before it reached its destination. Boxes containing clothes, sent by mothers to their sons and husbands in the army, were opened. The clothing these mothers had worked so hard to make was stolen, and replaced with rags and sent on its way. No one seemed to care.

Brokers bought cotton for ten cents a pound and sold it for one dollar. Quinine, upon which the Confederate army greatly depended, brokers purchased for fifty cents per pound and sold for two dollars an ounce.

Those men who had been discharged from the army as unfit beheld this lawlessness and decided to have a part in it. They brought river piracy back to New Orleans. The pirates did the same thing to the brokers that these gentlemen were doing to the Confederacy. The banker and broker, when confronted with this problem, went to the city authorities and complained bitterly. The police force, weakened by war, did all possible, but were unable to stop this practice.

Someone suggested that the police use Lafitte the Pirate's methods to bring this thieving under control. In fairness to Lafitte, this writer would like to say, Lafitte issued orders to Dominique You to stop such unlawful actions. Dominique also engaged, sent in his place a

Dago. It seems the Dago was also busy and did not care to waste time running down river thieves. After dark the Dago took several men in a skiff, rowed slowly along the riverfront and caught the thieves as they plied their trade. Those who fell into his hands were shown no mercy. With one stroke from the cutlass, the culprit's head fell into the skiff, his body was cast into the river. The following day the heads were stuck upon shortstakes which had been driven into a high floating log, with a sign attached: "Last night river rats—today what?" The log with its gruesome burden was allowed to drift past the city. In a very short time the Dago in his horrible, crude but effective manner stopped river piracy.

New Orleans police were not pirates and of course, could not apply such methods as the Dago. The police finally stopped this thievery, but not before it had spread to other Southern ports. The toll taken by this racket did much to put the Confederate army into the rags it wore.

From the day Louisiana seceded from the Union to the day reports that the Confederate armies were not faring so well, began to drift back, New Orleans was a gay place—she was indeed *The City Care Forgot.*

Sunday was the same as Monday. Hermes was her god and served her well. Disease, such as yellow fever, cholera, black vomit, and smallpox disappeared as if by magic. She wined, dined and danced upon the best money could buy. The Creole belles wore clothes and jewelry as did their sisters in the days before them when shopping was done at Barataria for contraband.

The hack driver charged one dollar per block and two dollars for the same distance when it was raining. The minimum bet in cheap resorts was five dollars; in classy places, one hundred dollars. Good whiskey in dives cost fifty cents per drink; in swanky places, two dollars per drink. The police grew so fat it was said of them that they were as big around as they were high up. Whiskey, love and money were plentiful. One could buy for one dollar and sell for ten. For the old city was out, the water fine and all swam in one grand carnival of exotic pleasure. Hermes was most liberal. The only sign of displeasure in New Orleans was found with the confessional priests. Their ears became tired from rest, their advice went begging. Their prayers: "May the day come that will end such living and bring the people back to their God and senses."

These prayers were answered in April, 1862, when the Federals announced a complete blockade of Confederate ports. Farragut, admiral of the Yankee fleet, was going to run the two forts below New Orleans. If he succeeded the old city would soon become a Yankee town. Farragut passed the forts and took New Orleans without firing a shot. The authorities did a little buck-passing and then surrendered the city.

With the coming of Farragut, New Orleans changed her flimsy red garments for sackcloth. Gold ceased to flow to her as the water to the sea, whiskey and love became cheap, confessional booths did a land office business and the old city staggered through the remaining period of the war as if blind and cared not whether she lived or died.

Silver Spoon Ben

Lazy New Orleans awoke the morning of April 26, 1862, to find the flagship of Admiral Farragut's federal fleet badly battered but still able to bombard the city, and waiting for the command to fire. This order never came, for New Orleans surrendered, and three days later Forts Jackson and St. Phillip, seventy-five miles below the city, surrendered to Porter, and New Orleans was a Yankee town.

One hundred and thirty-five years ago General Andrew Jackson stated, "New Orleans is the Nation's back door; whoever commands that door will soon command the Nation." the truth of this statement can be found in the history of the War of 1812, the Mexican War, Civil War, and Spanish-American War. The fall of New Orleans was the thrust that started Confederate blood to flow.

On May 1, 1862, Admiral Farragut retired and Benjamin F. Butler, a Yankee general, with fifteen thousand troops took command. The flag of Louisiana was lowered and the Stars and Stripes was raised. A few days after the lowering of the flag of Louisiana and the raising of the Stars and Stripes, Mumford, a young man, climbed the U. S. mint building and tore down the Union flag. General Butler ordered him to be hanged, and New Orleans, thereafter, for the better class of people, became a living hell.

Butler was a czar, from his decisions there was no appeal. Upon the pretense that he was the guardian angel of the poor, he robbed and confiscated. Of all the thieves that have entered New Orleans, Butler was by far the lowest. He entered a home as an honored guest and stole the silverware. The next day he issued the order and a squad of soldiers went to that home and confiscated all that Butler had not stolen. It was these acts that gained him the name "Silver Spoon Ben."

Butler made the St. Charles hotel his headquarters. That famous hostelry soon looked more like an office building of the War Department than a hotel. His stay here was short but active. The manager was driven almost to the point of madness by Butler's destructive, high-handed methods. The hotel was forced to accept Negroes as guests. In the lobby they loafed, drank and sang; the white guests, grossly insulted, left. The mezzanine became the scene of nightly parties given by Butler. At first ladies and gentlemen attended. When they learned that with Butler the Negro was their equal socially, they ignored his invitations. To this "snubbing," as Butler called it, he laughed, and to further antagonize the aristocrats he decreed that the yellow women were the city's elite. He, with his staff, entertained these women each evening. The majority of Butler's staff were honorable men and would have revolted at such rottenness had they not feared Butler's swift, brutal judgment. Instead, they smiled and told the general they enjoyed dining and dancing with these thick lipped women.

With the aid of Mayor Monroe of New Orleans, the hotel management induced General Butler to move his headquarters to the brick mansion on the corner of St. Charles and Julia streets. At first Butler refused. However, when he was told that the Negro officers of the Union army were complaining that the hotel was so crowded that they were unable to see him without hours of delay, Butler decided to vacate. The hotel manager waited until Butler was settled in his new quarters to send him his bill. Butler read it, smiled, and sent it back with a message that it would be a good idea for the hotel to receipt the bill paid, otherwise he might use it as quarters for his Negro staff. The hotel took the hint and checked the bill as paid.

Butler bought everything that was offered for sale, and paid for nothing. The yellow women who were forced to dance and dine all night were thrown out in the morning without compensation. These women soon grew weary of such treatment and as soon as the opportunity presented, they left town. Butler, his staff and soldiers noticed the scarcity of yellow women and began to turn their attention to the white women.

New Orleans' white womenfolk refused to speak to the officers and soldiers of the Union Army. To retaliate, the soldiers carried tales to General Butler that the white women openly insulted and displayed in various ways their contempt for them. Some reported that as they walked along the sidewalks, ladies from balconies would empty the contents of *pot-ala-chambre* upon them. The General became furious; not because the ladies showed their hatred but because there were no women for his parties. It was the latter which caused Butler to issue his world-notorious order, which reads in part: "Any woman who in anywise shows contempt for a Union officer or soldier will be arrested and tried on the charge of being a woman about town plying her trade." This order, known as No. 28, caused quite a stir in the capitals of Europe and nearly caused Butler's recall. Butler never relented and the order stood. Ladies on the streets, thereafter, turned their backs when passing Union officers and soldiers.

When this was reported to Butler, he laughed and said, "Those women evidently know which end of them looks the best." Not since the day Adam said the woman gave to me the fruit of the tree and I did eat, has such a cold, cruel, accusing remark been passed about women. The remark made by Benjamin F. Butler is considered the foulest utterance ever made by American man regarding women.

Again European and Northern women condemned Butler and almost forced his recall. President Lincoln overrode this objection and General Butler remained. It was of Butler that General Grant said, "What can one expect of a man who lives with a bottle and is fed with a spoon?"

So strong became Butler's hatred for New Orleans' better class of people that he inaugurated the scheme of raising the assessments upon people he disliked. In his ruthless hands this was a powerful weapon; however, it proved a boomerang for it became the source of his recall. Much to the delight of New Orleans, Butler was relieved of his command and General N. P. Banks, a refined, cultured, Northern gentleman, took his place.

For a week after his release, Butler remained. Some said it took a week for him to sober up, as he had not drawn a sober breath during his stay in the city. Others said Butler had not had a bath in so long his underwear clung to him so snugly it took a week of soaking in a Napoleon type bath tub to free the clinging parts.

Butler left New Orleans never to return. Neither did the silverware he took with him. The Creoles were most thankful that he did not take the Mississippi river. They celebrated his removal with an old-time ball, danced and dined to exotic music, with short prayers during intermissions that the hideous shadow of Silver Spoon Ben would never again darken their place in the world.

The Farmer General

The civilian population of the South, especially that of the larger cities, faced the approaching winter of 1862-63 with a mournful countenance. Food was scarce and prices high. This condition applied more to New Orleans than to any other, as she was the first city to fall. Since May 1, 1862, she had been a federal possession under the command of General Butler. The federal blockade stopped all supplies for New Orleans, and worked a terrible hardship upon the poor, many of whom would have died of starvation had not General Butler come to their rescue with food from the Union army rations. Unfortunately for the poor, General Butler was recalled in October, 1862, and General N. Prentiss Banks took command.

General Banks was born and reared on a poor New England farm. He had worked hard all his life and did not approve of feeding people who would not work. His first order was to stop the use of army rations for charity. If one wanted food, he must work for it. This order exploded like a bombshell in the midst of the city's unfortunate. They cursed General Banks for all they could think of, invoked the aid of voodoo queens and doctors, and prayed that all kinds of dreadful things would happen to him. The General's health, however, remained fine and his order of "No work, no food" stood.

Among the many horrors the natives of New Orleans have, hard work is most dreaded, for in that old city one is not judged by the company he keeps, but by the condition of the heart. For there, the man or woman who works is never looked down upon.

General Butler, while in command of the city, in a very feeble way decreed the natives should work, but put forth no effort to enforce it. The poor prayed for Butler's return and declared that they would rather have a silver thieving, nigger loving general than a Yankee slave driver.

New Orleans in 1862 consisted of several independent municipalities. The boundary lines between these two governments were large open canals eight to twelve feet deep, and twenty to thirty feet wide, with no outlets. They were for drainage purposes only. Later, however, they came to be used as sewers. New Orleans at that time had no sanitation board and what few sanitary laws she did have were not enforced. The old fashioned water closet was used. It was drained by a small ditch which ran alongside the house and emptied into a gutter that carried the refuse into the canal where it remained until disposed of by the elements.

General Banks looked the city over to find some gainful employment for the unfortunates. He finally decided he would finish what General Butler had attempted. This was to stop the canals and street gutters from being used as sewers. He condemned the canals and gutters and began filling them and in their place he inaugurated the container and lime system. Once every two weeks Negroes would call and empty the containers into barrels; the contents were hauled to the swamps and there dumped.

General Banks formed a committee to see that the work was done and to plan other means of drainage. From this order issued by General Banks, New Orleans' sewerage and water board was born. In the following two and one-half years the committee worked hard and did much towards eliminating this evil.

The Civil War ended, much to the satisfaction of all. New Orleans, after a check on Southern cities, was found to have fared better in foods and medicines than any other part of the South.

In viewing one of New Orleans' many wide, modern, paved avenues of today, lined with magnificent homes, trees, palms and flowers, one would not think that only a few years ago it was a foul, vile-smelling, disease spreading open sewer. Perhaps this condition would have remained much longer than it did had it not been for the Civil War and a Yankee general who said "if you want food you must work for it."

The Bitter Return

April ninth, 1865, the First Artillery fired the last shot of the Civil War. General Robert E. Lee had surrendered at Appomattox, and the War of Blood, listed in history as the 893rd war since 600 B. C., was at an end. Thus ended the bloodiest slaughter of human beings in the history of man. It lacked exactly three days of lasting four years.

Of the 900,000 men who fought under the Confederate Flag, 129,195 lay buried somewhere. The remainder, tired, barefooted, ragged, half-starved, started on the long trek home. They passed through states that were once happy and prosperous. Now, this territory looked like a land over which savages had roamed. Many were the veterans who wiped their eyes upon what was once a coat sleeve. Each gritted his teeth and plodded on to receive at the journey's end one of the bitterest pills man occasionally is forced to swallow; a pill so bitter it brought a lump to the throat and shriveled the heart, whereby their crying prayers needed not the onetime coat sleeve. What suffering, hardships and humiliation the wives, children, aged parents and other dear ones must have undergone! The battlefield was child's play compared to the conditions the Confederate soldier found at home.

News did not travel as fast in those days as now. Word of General Lee's surrender did not reach New Orleans until after President Lincoln called upon Congress to consider plans for rehabilitating the South. Unfortunately for the South, especially New Orleans, five days after Lee's surrender President Lincoln was assassinated and the South lost the iron hand that would have been her friend. Johnson, who succeeded Lincoln, was helpless against the South's two most outstanding political foes. Senators Summers and Stevens. New Orleans mourned the passing of Lincoln, but not for long. She soon was started upon a round of gaiety, celebrating the war's end.

Her balls, for which she was once famous, were now called, due to the lack of cocktails and mint julips, "starvation balls." This shortage of tongue-loosening and moral-lowering drinks worked a hardship upon the gay and dashing blades. Although there were a few who could afford such, they were afraid and kept their drinking confined to extreme privacy lest it be said of them that they were slackers who stayed at home and sold cotton to the Yankees. Once this remark became gossip, that person was forever black-balled from New Orleans' polite society. The badge of the aristocrat was poverty and was worn without shame.

The federal blockade had been removed, but prices remained high. In fact, for the first year after the war prices were much higher, e. g., flour sold for $150 per barrel, salt meat for $20 per pound. Whiskey, the only cure for yellow fever, if used in time, was $60 per quart. Of course this was the cost in Confederate money. There was very little Federal money in Louisiana in the first year after the war, Senators Summers and Stevens saw to that. To these exorbitant prices New Orleans lifted high her foul-smelling skirts and shook them at this calamity as she did the many others she had overcome.

June, 1865, there came from Washington an order to evacuate Federal soldiers from the city proper and turn the city over to the new-forming metropolitan policc which was headed by the carpet-baggers. At first, the natives thought this was a blessing; however, they soon learned differently. The poor white trash and Negroes from East Texas, Arkansas, Mississippi and Louisiana thought this was the time and place the Yankees were going to divide this section of the South. These people believed that the Yankees would give to each family forty acres and a mule. In this they were badly fooled. The carpetbaggers who arrived ahead of them, well armed with authority from a Yankee Congress, swindled these unfortunates out of whatever claims they may have had. This was the first act of the carpetbaggers in Louisiana.

The second act of these gentlemen was to mortgage the land and sell the mules up the river. The proceeds they placed in an Eastern bank and prepared for several years of undisturbed plunder. Negroes overran the city. They were immune from arrest. Their food was paid for with Louisiana money, furnished by the carpet bag government, while many of the native whites were forced to live out of garbage cans from the Union army camps. Many Federal soldiers felt sorry and smuggled food to them when possible. The whites in their prayers exclaimed, "This is worse than war."

Under the carpet bag rule New Orleans grew more and more bitter day by day. Her actions, her talk, her prayers were full and overflowing with bitterness. This bitterness slowly turned into hatred; she endured and endured until she could endure no longer. Late in the year 1874, her pent-up hatred burst loose like a toy balloon and she struck like a rattlesnake, most effectively but not without warning and the political organization in New Orleans known today as the Old Regulars was born—and still exists.

The Bone Pile

Throughout the world there are many, varied and curious ways of disposing of the dead. In the mountains of Abyssinia is a people who believe a man should be buried where he dies without pomp or ceremony; neither should the remains be moved from the exact site of death one foot more than necessary.

This practice is thousands of miles away; let us come to our own country, and in New Orleans we find another queer, unique mode of burial. In order to more clearly understand this mode of burial, we should first know something of her cemeteries, which are more than thirty in number.

New Orleans has the country's oldest cemetery, (St. Louis No. 1), with an area of about one and one-half acres and an estimated ninety thousand burials, all above ground. It is correctly called "A City of the Dead," and is still used today.

This unique way of interment was not by choice but by necessity. In the days before artificial drainage the water table was within a foot of the surface, therefore a standard grave was out of the question. The problem was solved with the present system—a cross between the catacombs of Rome and a mode used by the inhabitants of the lowlands along the Northern Mediterranean Sea.

Of all New Orleans' cemeteries, St. Louis No. 1, due to age and quaintness, is the most interesting. It has one entrance, facing east, so small a casket has to be carried, or wheeled in . The streets, lanes or passageways between the vaults are paved with shell, they are narrow and none too straight and often blind, with an occasional pomegranite or magnolia tree.

Most of the vaults have two and four compartments, called crypts or ovens. They are privately owned and as a rule, kept in a fair state of repair. Others, from the lack of proper foundations, have sunk practically beneath the surface, some have sunk on one side so far they could easily be toppled over. Then there are the large vaults, having twenty-four to thirty compartments. These are erected by societies of the city. The fence or wall which encloses the cemetery forms what is called the wall vaults and in these are buried the poorer classes. The wall vaults are four compartments high, and are erected, sold and rented by the church.

Many of these compartments have a small balcony the length of the opening, approximately thirty inches.

On these balconies are placed flower pots, vases and small pieces of marble, usually with only one word inscribed: Mother, Father, Wife, Sister or Brother. Those which do not have balconies may have a wooden shelf. Some have neither, their only ornament a home-made tin flower pot which looks like a funnel cut in half. In the cracks and on top of the vaults where dust has settled grows a species of fern and occasionally a species of narcissus, the Star of Bethlehem.

As to how one is buried, let us follow the sexton as he prepares a vault for use. Into a wheelbarrow he places a shovel, rake and a heavy hammer with a short handle. If it is a top vault he places the wheelbarrow in front of it and stands in it. In the event the vault has not been opened for a score or more years, he hesitates, thinks, wonders, and, who knows? there may be buried treasure. Then, with gentle blows he loosens the brick and takes them out one by one, pausing to clean each, as they are to be used again to seal the vault.

The moving of the first brick lets in the light and suddenly a buzzing sound is heard which is followed by an exodus of bright bronze-colored roaches. Occasionally there is quite a commotion within the vault. This is caused by a rat running over loose bones and usually making its escape, as the sexton is by this time busily fighting roaches off his person.

Holding his nose and shading his eyes, the sexton peers into the vault and looks at the future as far as it is possible. What he sees he will never forget.

The interiors of the vaults are not always the same. If the vault has not been opened in many years, the casket will have fallen in decay, leaving the skeleton intact lying flat on the vault floor. Amid the casket's remains occasionally a skeleton has been found face down, indicating some one had been buried alive, which was not unusual years ago. The people had such a horror of this that it was customary to place a bell in the hand of the corpse.

The sexton draws the skull to him with the rake and smiles or shakes his head, for at one time medical students paid ten dollars for a good skull; then, too, some people filled their teeth with gold. He searches the vault and with the rake pushes the remains back into a corner, where, as a rule, is a small, neat pile of bones.

The next vault opened may have been used in the last two or three years. In this instance, the greeting is different, for the casket is found in good shape if not too cheap. The sexton then takes his time removing the cover. This accomplished, the casket is turned upside down so the remains may fall out. When the roach episode, which lasts about two minutes, is over, the casket is placed in the sun to dry. The vault is then searched and the bones pushed back into the corner. It is in instances of this kind that one can see that the hair, toe and finger nails grow after death. When the sexton opens a vault and finds the casket in such condition that it has no value, it is burned. The remains in a rented vault, when the rent has not been paid, are taken out and buried.

A vault can be purchased, or rented for a year and a day. According to law this much time must elapse before the vault can be opened. By this time there is nothing left to a body but bones. As many as thirty-odd people have been buried in the same vault or crypt. Should two members of a family die within a year, a vault is rented for a year and a day for the second member and after that time the remains can be transferred to the family vault. This is done to save rent for many Orleanians, like other people, believe it is cheaper to move than to pay rent.

In most of the city's cemeteries the line of creed or color is not drawn, Jew, Catholic, Mason, Protestant, white and black are buried side by side. This mode of burial applies to rich and poor alike. There are, of course, some exceptions, but the majority of the people of New Orleans believe this is the proper way to inter their dead.

Yellow Jack

Yellow fever, a most dreaded disease, is characteristic of the western tropic. Because of it, Louisiana is noted for its great charitable, medical institutions and New Orleans the medical center of the western hemisphere. In 1796 New Orleans had its first recognized outbreak of this quick-working malady. For lack of funds she was unable to cope with an epidemic and no doubt Yellow Jack would have depopulated the city had it not been for a Spanish nobleman, Don Almonaster, who purchased a building and founded the western world's first charity hospital. There, those who were afflicted with Yellow Jack were confined.

The city's learned European physicians were at a loss as to the cause or cure for Yellow Jack. People died like flies while the doctors pulled their hair and searched their medical books and brains for some effective remedy. Yellow Jack, as though controlled by witches and fairies, left like it came, leaving misery and debt, but no one the wiser.

Again, in 1801, New Orleans was visited by Yellow Jack. Her Latin blood fell easy victim. The medical men once more searched brains and books, but to no avail. People died faster than they could be buried, and bodies decomposing in the streets added to the horror.

Such was the condition when some one suggested

the city's physicians consult Syrile Ramiyon, the Doctor of Honey Isle. These gentlemen scoffed at the idea of consulting a quack, as they called Syrile Ramiyon. In desperation, however, they swallowed their pride and ethics and called the Doctor of Honey Isle. Immediately, Syrile Ramiyon informed them that yellow fever was caused by the bite of the mosquito which was bred in filth. His advice was to clean up the city and Yellow Jack will disappear forever.

The physicians laughed and said, "Absurd." Because they refused to heed the Doctor of Honey Isle's suggestion, New Orleans for ninety-nine years fought Yellow Jack with little help from the state and none from the federal government.

Washington had no interest in Yellow Jack until an epidemic broke out among soldiers in Cuba during the Spanish-American war. American physicians were likewise lost as to treatment and cause of this scourge. They consulted a native physician, who said he knew no cure but did know the cause—bites from the mosquito bred in stagnant water. Again the American doctors laughed and wanted to know from whence came the idea. He smilingly answered, "Nearly a hundred years ago Doctor Syrile Ramiyon, a Louisianian, advanced the theory and I have to my own satisfaction proved it to be correct."

Among these American army doctors was one Walter Reed, who, for lack of a better theory, accepted this one and proved it true. Soldiers in quarantine called the fever by the same name the Baratarian pirates gave it, Yellow Jack. The pirates gave it the name because they said the mosquito had a yellow spot on the underside of its body.

Yellow Jack was the scourge of New Orleans for more than a hundred and fifty years. During this time she endured several great epidemics. One of the last was shortly after the Civil War when several thousand people died in less than three weeks. Suffering and want became almost unbearable—well today, sick tomorrow, and a corpse the following day. Yellow Jack worked fast; first one felt badly, next a headache, then a chill, fever followed, vomiting came, then the body turned yellow and invariably the end was death, all within twenty-four hours, unless one had expert medical care.

Today a man was well, taking care of his wife. Tomorrow he was ill and the wife dead. Smallpox Negroes (one who has had smallpox) came, wrapped the body of the dead in sheets, placed the remains on what the Negroes called "Ox bow corpse carrier." And carried it out, cast it upon a wagon loaded with other such bodies. When the wagon was filled, the Negroes drove it to the "dead church" which stands on the corner of Rampart and Conti streets. There the bodies were piled upon the sidewalk, the wagon driven to the rear of the church, the priest said a few words, and the bodies were again loaded on the wagon. White, black, Catholic, Jew and Protestant all were treated alike. This procedure continued day and night seemingly without end. The loaded wagon proceeded to the cemetery were hundreds of other bodies were piled like cordwood upon the sidewalks. Here other smallpox Negroes had large sugar boilers filled with hot tar. As the bodies were stacked, hot tar was poured over them. This done, first to kill the odor, and second, to prevent the buzzards which lined the cemetery walls from feasting.

Time was too precious to be wasted in digging six feet into the ground to bury the bodies. Accordingly, the wall vaults were used, where three or four were forced into one compartment with a ram. Burying in the ground was impossible; at the depth of three feet water was struck. Digging, then, was very slow. A victim of Yellow Jack must be interred at least six feet, otherwise the horrible fetor of decomposing flesh leaked out. Such was the way in which victims of Yellow Jack were treated.

This disease is no more. The old city has not had an epidemic in years. Yellow Jack caused the city much suffering and carried off more of her people than all the wars in which she has participated. It became the foundation upon which was built her just claim of the medical center of the western world.

Yellow Jack gave New Orleans the highest death rate in the country. Today it is among the lowest. No more does water stand on her streets for days after a rain.

Only the old speak of Yellow Jack. The young know nothing of it. New Orleans has so cleaned herself, Yellow Jack remains only in her history and the minds of the aged. Today, where disease is concerned, New Orleans is one of the world's cleanest cities. Otherwise, as tradition says, she still loves to dress in red and cling to her old emblem, an apple with one bite missing.

An ox-bow corpse carrier.

Where North Is South

Continental United States has but four distinctive cities with an atmosphere of their own. Of this group we find New Orleans the crowning jewel. With her many peculiarities she is rightly called America's most interesting city.

The first bit of her uniqueness the visitor comes in contact with is the cardinal points. Almost everyone has studied, read or been told that New Orleans is on the east bank of the Mississippi river. This is correct.

In the morning, as is the custom, many visitors walk to the foot of Canal street and the river. To their surprise they see the sun as it rises from the opposite shore over the little city of Algiers, and immediately conclude this is wrong: New Orleans is certainly on the west side of the river. On second thought, however, one reasoned this cannot be true, for he came from the east and at no time had he crossed the river. As a rule, the visitor struggles with this problem until a dock board officer comes along and cheerfully explains the situation as follows:

The Mississippi river at the foot of Canal street flows due north, completing a graceful fourteen-mile bend or curve, or, as the native says, the crescent. In this lies the greater part of New Orleans and explains the name of Crescent City. Although New Orleans is east of the river, at this point, due to the crescent, the city appears to be on the west side. As one stands at the foot of Canal street that which appears to be the west bank is in reality the east bank. This is the cause of the confusion among those who are not natives. It is this particular bend in the river which causes the native to say New Orleans is the only place in the world where the sun rises in the west and sets in the east. This also accounts for the fact that New Orleans has no north, south, east or west side. If she had, the visitor would have even more difficulty getting about, for the west side would be the east side, the north side would be the south side, and vice versa. Instead of the above, the native has substituted Uptown for south, Downtown for north, Intown for along the river, and Back of Town for the west side.

Canal street is the dividing line between north and south. It is a scant four miles in length, 171 feet wide, the banquette or sidewalks 18 feet wide, traffic lanes are 37½ feet, the neutral ground is 60 feet wide. At one time the neutral ground was an open canal, from which came the street's name.

For ten blocks from the river, streets which intersect Canal street change names at the intersection. This, together with the streets' peculiar names, creates more confusion. Then there are the one-way streets, many of which are narrow and are often taken for alleys, which adds to the troubles of those who are trying to find their way about town. One would ordinarily suppose that if a street is one way to the right, the next would be to the left. This, however, is not always true. For the benefit of the street cars, two streets in succession may be right or left turns. As a result one often finds himself in a traffic jam caused by one who is not familiar with the city's queer system of one-way streets.

Should one park his car and start walking, he would fare little better, for two and three streets come together and form one. Blind streets and streets which run in a circle soon cause the pedestrian to become lost, even within a few blocks of his hotel. The native, if asked, will usually give directions by saying so many squares up, and so many squares in, or out. This, of course, means little to one who is not familiar with the terms "in town," and "back of town," etc. This situation is cleared if the pedestrian continues to ask questions; if not, he continues to wander anxiously around until he stumbles into a policeman or, if in a hurry, he finds it much more convenient to hail a taxi to rescue him.

This explains, in part, why it is so easy to become confused and lose one's sense of direction in New Orleans.

The Brigham Young Courtyard

The Brigham Young Courtyard, or as painters, etchers and other artists call the place, "Clothespole Alley", is situated at number 724 on the south side of the ancient thoroughfare of Hospital Street (since renamed Governor Nicholls).

The U-shaped building consists of two floors, and was erected by the Spanish shortly after Spain took possession of Louisiana in 1768.

In Spain cavalry was an important branch of the armed services. The Spanish were far greater believers in horse flesh than the military of any other European power ever to claim a portion of the New World. They erected the building to stable the fine horses which were ridden by the army officers.

The unique construction of the building was for the purpose of stabling the horses on the ground floor and furnishing living quarters for the animal attendants on the second.

The name, "Clothespole Alley", results from the fact that the women who occupy the place cannot hang out the family wash on the ground floor, whereby their clothes may be dried in the sun. Hence the women, on special made clotheslines, string the wash along the second floor gallery (porch) post, and swing the clothes out over the courtyard with long poles, high above the heads of both man and beast. Because of the many poles used, the artists dubbed it "The Clothespole Alley."

When Jean Lafitte, the so-called Pirate of Barataria, (Pronounced By-er-tear-er-ya), took over all activities at this pirate's roost of the Mexican Gulf north coast line, one of the first things he learned was that Barataria needed a blacksmith badly.

At the time, however, good blacksmiths were not any too plentiful in this section of the country, so not to waste time, Lafitte fetched one over from France. Shortly after the arrival of the French smithy, an incident occurred which plainly demonstrated to Lafitte that he would not be able to keep a good blacksmith at Barataria.

The French iron worker had no more than got his shop set up and functioning, when into the place came an English pirate, with a bent cutlass, two pistols in his belt, and far too much whiskey under said belt, and in a terrible hurry to have the cutlass straightened.

The 'smith argued that he could not have the cutlass ready for several days. The pirate said that he must have the weapon by morning, and he emphasized his request by laying the cutlass on the anvil, and taking a long hardy swig from a jug suspended from his shoulder by a strap, placed a well directed bullet between the blacksmith's feet. As he staggered out of the shop, he shouted:

"I'll be back at daylight for my weapon."

The next morning found the blacksmith a long way from Barataria, with Lafitte determined to move the shop to New Orleans. In another's name, Lafitte rented the Brigham Young Courtyard, then known as the Spanish Stable Courtyard. He converted the place into a blacksmith shop which soon became known as "Lafitte's Blacksmith Shop." It bore that title until the latter part of the year 1844.

Early in June of the year 1844, the members of the Mormon Church of Carthage, Illinois, got into trouble with the citizens of that community, and the church elders along with their supreme leader, Joseph Smith, were cast into prison.

Bright and early on the morning of June 27, 1844, a mob stormed the jail and killed Joseph Smith and his brother Hiram. Shortly after this incident the Elders of the Mormon Church elected Brigham Young, their supreme leader.

The oath of office had barely cleared the tongue of Brigham Young, when he awakened to the fact that he had assumed a terrific responsibility. Flowers of "want" immediately began to bloom about his head, and the odor thereof nauseated his power of reason. Turning a wooden ear to the cries of his fellowmen, he took to the forest, where in silent prayer, he walked among the trees, pulling his long tresses, seemingly in useless effort, seeking an answer to the awful predicament in which he now found himself.

The great Mormon leader was as fine a man as ever trod our soil, and one of the greatest leaders our nation has ever produced, but he was a worried man. The Mormons were a healthy lot and blessed with enormous appetites, but little food. From the lack of chicken, fried or otherwise, the elders rent their hair and cursed their day.

Brigham Young, however, heard neither their curses nor lamentations. He remained in the woods all day and night. On the morning of the second day his mind went blank. All about him became dark—dark as though the mantle of Elijah had suddenly shrouded his head, leaving him in total darkness.

This unusual phenomenon, however, was for but a moment's duration. His mind cleared, and then as a shaft of frightful lightning from an evil sky, two thoughts entered the fertile brain of Brigham Young. Both were as a prophet's dream, and seemingly as futile. He accepted both as revelations and immediately added action to the acceptance.

First, he would dispatch a letter to Tontoe, explaining the Mormon's sad plight and asking for help. Tontoe, a river racketeer, operating out of Natchez, owed his life to the Mormons. The Mormons had once saved Tontoe's neck from being stretched by an angry group of Missouri riders. For the saving of his neck, Tontoe, promised the Mormons, if there ever came a time that he could help them, all they had to do was to call upon him.

While waiting for the messenger to return, Brigham Young organized the Mormons for the long march to Council Bluffs. This point, if Tontoe could aid him, would be the jumping off place to the valley of the great Salt Lake. The long, dangerous trek, he planned to make with covered wagons. But wagons, covered or not, were among the many things the Mormons did not possess. Timber and tools necessary to build wagons they had. Iron for wagon-wheel rims and hubs, however, was as scarce as brotherly love in Carthage.

The messenger returned with a most favorable reply. Tontoe's letter stated that he had $5,000 in gold, plenty of guns, ammunition, and blankets—all of which the Mormons might have on an hour's notice. Brigham Young waited no longer. Under the command of an Elder, he sent the Mormons on their way to Council Bluffs, and with two Elders he started for Natchez, pushing their horses as much as they dared.

Tontoe, not only gave Brigham Young the gold, but also a letter of introduction to the blacksmith operating the shop at the Spanish Stable Courtyard in New Orleans, when the Mormon leader mentioned how great was their need for iron wagon wheel rims.

For five weeks, from "Can see to can't see," Brigham Young, under the blacksmith's supervision, with the aid of the two Elders and a few Negroes, made the iron hubs and wheel rims that the Mormons used on their trek to the far west.

Brigham Young and his Elders arrived in New Orleans the first week in August, which is the city's hottest month. With the days hot and the forge hotter, Young occasionally would step out on the banquette (side-walk) for a bit of fresh air. While cooling his body and refreshing his lungs, he could hear the Creole gentlemen, bitterly complain about the narrow streets and their carriages forever being held up by some vehicle, or other.

The rims, sufficient for 19 wagons, the blacksmith said were made in a record time. They were loaded into three purchased wagons, together with other necessities. Brigham Young knowing full well that about the only thing a Mormon could purchase in Illinois was a dose of poison, did considerable shopping before leaving New Orleans. A day or so before he departed he was asked to talk on Mormonism. The Creole gentlemen very much approved of the Mormon's home life, and wanted to know more of his religion. The great Mormon leader refused to make a talk and said: "For a Mormon, in New Orleans to make a talk on his church would be like throwing a fat sheep to a starved wolf pack in the dead of winter."

Brigham Young quit New Orleans, never to return, but his visit to the Crescent City he never forgot. When he drew the plans for the delightful city of Salt Lake, Utah, he remembered the Creoles' bitter complaints about the narrow streets of the French Quarter, and declared, "That will never happen here."

It was not long after the departure of Brigham Young, before the old folks in the "Quarter" began calling the Lafitte Blacksmith Shop, "The Brig'em Young Court."

The Civil War came and ended, and with the ending came the Yankee Fancy Boys (carpet baggers). These "boys" being Yankees could not relish anything pertaining to Mormonism, and ordered all who persisted in calling the Lafitte Blacksmith Shop, the Brigham Young Court, to have their heads stuck in the mud. This decree soon stopped the calling of the courtyard by that name, and it reverted back to its first title—Spanish Stable Courtyard. It remained as such until the coming of the artists who dubbed it "Clothespole Alley."

Conclusion

Prior to the Louisiana Purchase, in conversation with James Monroe, Secretary of State, President Thomas Jefferson said: "Louisiana at fifteen million dollars is a bargain, but where in the name of the Almighty God are we to get the money." Jefferson, however, with the aid of his friend. Anselm Rothschild got the money, and U. S., Louisiana. Shortly thereafter Jefferson made the following statement: "If New Orleans will forsake her old world laws, customs and habits, she within the century will be one of the world's largest cities."

Nearly a century and a half have passed since Jefferson made this statement. During this time many cities have not only come into existence, but have far surpassed New Orleans in population, building and enterprise. Many reasons have been advanced as to why, but the most logical one is: "Her love for an exotic life, rather than a commercial one."

To the visitor, drunk or sober, New Orleans extends most heartily her never changing welcome sign—"The door is open; the dog is tied." Likewise, as it is soon learned, her motto, "Nothing ventured; nothing gained, has never changed.

[THE END]

Lear Navard, the author's son, aged nine, standing by the head of a voodoo idol.

STORIES of NEW ORLEANS